Inclusive Education, Politics and Policymaking

Also available in the Contemporary Issues in Education Studies Series

Changing Urban Education, Simon Pratt-Adams, Meg Maguire and
  Elizabeth Burn
Education and Constructions of Childhood, David Blundell
Multiculturalism and Education, Richard Race
New Technology and Education, Anthony Edwards
Young People, Popular Culture and Education, Chris Richards

Also available from Continuum

Education Policy, Practice and the Professional, Jane Bates, Sue Lewis and
  Andy Pickard
Rethinking the Education Improvement Agenda, Kevin J. Flint and Nick Peim

Inclusive Education, Politics and Policymaking

Contemporary Issues in Education Studies

Anastasia Liasidou

continuum

Continuum International Publishing Group

The Tower Building	80 Maiden Lane
11 York Road	Suite 704
London SE1 7NX	New York NY 10038

www.continuumbooks.com

British Library Cataloguing-in-Publication Data
A catalogue record for this book is available from the British Library.

ISBN: 978-1-4411-5739-3 (paperback)
       978-1-4411-0901-9 (hardcover)

Library of Congress Cataloging-in-Publication Data
Liasidou, Anastasia.
Inclusive education, politics and policymaking / Anastasia Liasidou. –1
    p. cm. – (Contemporary issues in education studies)
Summary: "A critical overview on the history of inclusive education policy and practice developments, with suggestions for possible ways forward"– Provided by publisher.

ISBN 978-1-4411-5739-3 (pbk.) – ISBN 978-1-4411-0901-9 (hardcover) – ISBN 978-1-4411-5969-4 (ebook (epub))   1. Inclusive education.
    I. Title.   II. Series.
LC1200.L53 2012

371.9'046--dc23
2011029898

Typeset by Newgen Imaging Systems Pvt Ltd, Chennai, India
Printed and bound in India

Contents

Acknowledgements

The author gratefully acknowledges the help of Richard Race and Simon Pratt-Adams.

Series Editors' Preface

The series *Contemporary Issues in Education Studies* is timely for its critical exploration of education in this period of accelerating change. Responding to this challenge, the books in the series have titles which correspond closely to the needs of students taking a wide range of courses and modules within Education Studies and related fields such as teacher education. Education Studies is an important subject area that should be at the heart of many faculties of education. There is a need for relevant core texts within Education Studies which explore and critique contemporary issues across the discipline and challenge prevailing discourses of what education is about. We also need to provide students with strong theoretical perspectives and frameworks, focusing on relevant literature in an accessible and readable format.

We set the authors of this series a number of challenges in terms of what to include in their text. Therefore, each book addresses a contemporary issue in education and has an international rather than just an English focus. The texts are structured to provide a clear grasp of the topic and to provide an overview of research, current debates and perspectives. Contextualized extracts from important primary texts ensure readers' exposure to dominant contemporary theories in the field of education, by demystifying essential vocabulary and educational discourse, and enabling the education student to engage with these texts in a meaningful way. The extensive and appropriate literature review in each text gives a firm base for contextualizing the subject and promoting understanding at multiple levels.

This series is grounded in a strong conceptual, theoretical framework and is presented in an accessible way. Each book uses approaches such as case studies, reflective exercises and activities that encourage and support student learning. Key relevant and contemporary questions are inserted throughout each chapter to extend the readers' thinking and understanding. Furthermore, additional material is also provided in the companion website to each book.

Anastasia Liasidou is Assistant Professor in Inclusive Education in the School of Arts and Education Sciences at the European University, Nicosia, Cyprus. Her work has included research with the Training and Development Agency for Schools (TDA) in England about strengthening Special Educational

Needs (SEN) expertise among teachers. Her research interests include not only SEN-Disability, but cross-cultural and cross-disciplinary research into inclusive education policy and practice. Liasidou has published widely, including in international, peer-reviewed journals such as *the International Studies in Sociology of Education and the Journal of Education Policy*. For this book, Liasidou draws upon her own professional practice as an educator and an advocate for the promotion and extension of inclusive education policies for all children as well as her active engagement with research.

The book explores the historical and current importance and complexity of inclusion and educational policy-making: this is both a timely and welcome addition to the study of a sometimes controversial area of education. From a starting point of defining different perspectives of inclusion, the author offers a theoretical examination of the key issues relating to special education and their relevance for inclusive pedagogies. Liasidou offers a critical analysis of SEN-Disability policy-making which enables the reader to locate this area within a contemporary context. She offers a new perspective on special education drawing upon the social theorization of Weber and Bourdieu, and in particular Foucault.

Using sociological analysis the book explores the contested notions of ideology, power and control, and the interplay of these within political and institutional structures and action. The author examines cross-cultural and international perspectives; as with all books in this series, the reader is challenged to think about the relationship between global, national and local dimensions, in order to understand inclusion as the key to personalizing learning for all and teaching in the diverse classroom.

This book encourages the reader to analyse and reflect on the notion of inclusive education and consider how policy shapes and addresses inclusive conditions and practices. The continued promotion and extension of SEN-Disability and broader inclusive issues across education remain a major area of enquiry and research for educators and professionals across disciplines. We believe this book will make a significant contribution to the debates and become a major resource for all those interested in studying and researching inclusive education politics and policy-making.

Simon Pratt-Adams and Richard Race
August 2011
London and Athens

Introduction

The notions of inclusion and educational policymaking are both contested and multilayered. The understanding of the plurality of meanings ascribed to inclusion requires a thorough understanding of the processes and outcomes of inclusive educational policymaking. This entails analysing and exemplifying the complex and contested nature of educational policymaking, which is intertwined with and resting upon wider socio-political, historical and institutional considerations.

While drawing on some widely debated issues around inclusive education, the aim of the book is to analyse the multidimensional process of inclusive education policymaking by dissecting the struggles and dynamics that give rise to ambiguous and contradictory inclusive education policy landscapes characterized by incompatible perspectives and understandings, and explain the ways in which these perspectives and understandings have come into being and have become consolidated. The conceptual plurality underpinning the notion of inclusion calls for a critical and interdisciplinary approach capable of tracing and examining the provenance of a wide range of dynamics and socio-political exigencies that bring to bear a profound influence on how inclusion is conceptualized, understood and acted upon across time and space.

The multiple dilemmas underpinning inclusive education policy and practice mirror, amongst other things, the theoretical tensions of disability studies that have polarized the field (Oliver, 1996a; Corker and French, 1999; Thomas, 2004; Shakespeare, 1997; 2006). These theoretical contestations have been reconfigured to a string of vexed dilemmas with regard to the optimal ways in which 'difference' should be conceptualized and acted upon in current schooling (Norwich, 2008a). At the same time, the mere existence of these dilemmas raises serious questions as to who defines 'difference', how it is defined, under what conditions and what it means. Bearing in mind the arbitrary and contextual ways in which the notion of 'difference' has been constructed and theorized, arbitrations and assertions of what constitutes 'difference' call for a broader theoretical discussion and debate, something that this book aims to contribute towards.

Inclusive education policy and practice is also contingent on an array of dynamics pertaining to varied conceptualizations of students' diversity, abilities, learning, emotional development, human rights, citizenship and social justice (Barton, 1993; Artiles et al., 2006; Wedell, 2008; Rayner, 2009; Terzi, 2010), and is ushered in by a host of vexed dilemmas endemic to the systematic rigidities of current schooling that undermine attempts towards transformative change (Wedell, 2005, 2008; Slee, 2011).

The complicated and contested nature of inclusive education policymaking calls for theoretical and analytical openness and convergence, and entails raising questions and providing a critical analysis of the assumptions, ideas and related practices within the field. To this end, the book draws on an eclectic confluence of theoretical perspectives and analytical insights in order to critically interrogate key issues underpinning the complex processes and contentious outcomes of inclusive education policymaking. It attempts to question and destabilize individual deficit imperatives that have traditionally held sway over special education, thereby providing alternative theorizations of inclusive education policymaking, conceptualized in terms of the interplays of unequal power relations (Foucault, 1980a,b). The 'crises' and 'settlements' (Grace, 1991) characterizing the policymaking process are explicated as being invariably linked with the power/knowledge nexus which set the conceptual framework within which special education imperatives have emerged, become consolidated and reinvented through more inclusive veneers. The varied facets of unequal power relations informing the policymaking process are discussed and analysed within an interactive network consisting of micro and macro dynamics that constitute complex and multidimensional inclusive education policy landscapes.

The processes and outcomes of inclusive educational policymaking are explained as being the result of multiple struggles and unequal power relations central to which is the necessity to understand the ways in which language, discourse and institutional conditions intersect and give rise to a contradictory policy terrain, both in terms of official and enacted policies. The notions of language, discourses and institutional conditions are explored and contextualized within the interplay of agents and structures, against the backdrop of the varied struggles to initiate educational change and promote inclusion. A thorough analysis of these issues will provide a comprehensive understanding of the profusion of interconnections, interdependencies and consequential effects that render inclusion a highly political and difficult pursuit.

The book attests to the necessity of constantly and diligently interrogating the interactive framework of hierarchical, oppressive and discriminatory ideologies, politics and policies in the pursuit of inclusion. In this respect, it is suggested that the critical dimension of policy studies should be established as an indispensable element in the attempts towards transformative change. This is pursued by adopting a critical approach aimed at deconstructing the convoluted nature of inclusive educational policymaking and exploring a wide range of dynamics and contestations inherent in it. The critical dimension of policy analysis and its importance in understanding inclusion are thoroughly rationalized and explained, and implications for educational practice are discussed and reflected upon. Context and time specific national educational policy 'snapshots' are provided, so as to put abstract ideas and theorizations into practice, and provide instances of the intricate interplays of power underpinning the processes of policy constitution and dissemination.

1

Perspectives on Inclusion: Discourses, Politics and Educational Practice

Chapter Outline

Introduction

The chapter explores the different theoretical and policy interpretations of inclusion and analyses the ways in which a vast array of ideological and institutional dynamics are played out, contested and struggled over during the policymaking process. Given the multiplicity of the dynamics underpinning inclusive education policymaking, inclusion has been conceptualized and construed in varied ways, and has engendered multiple theoretical tensions and vexed dilemmas (Wedell, 2005; Norwich, 2008a).

Current versions of inclusion and implications for educational practice are discussed and analysed against the backdrop of broader theoretical discussions and debates. For instance, policy initiatives in the United Kingdom promote versions of inclusion aligned to the standards agenda, aimed to provide educational excellence irrespective of educational placement (Dyson, 2001,

2005). This contradictory policy terrain, which foregrounds both 'inclusion' and 'excellence' (the latter seen to be denoted almost exclusively by exam results and subsequent school league table rankings), creates tensions for schools in attempting to integrate two different and inherently contradictory agendas, namely the standards and inclusive education agendas (Barton and Armstrong, 2007). Related to this, the notion of social inclusion is used as a means to maximize the economic and social usefulness of 'docile bodies' (Foucault, 1979: 138), thereby ignoring the cultural politics of inclusion and special educational needs (Armstrong, 2005). New forms of inclusion, conjured up in terms of a deficit based approach, are discussed and critiqued. It is argued that these new forms of inclusion consolidate and perpetuate the notion of 'special educational needs' and the paraphernalia of assimilationist approaches of cure and remedy associated with it, thereby 'collapsing inclusive education into a concern with special educational needs' (Slee, 2011: 122).

The reduction of inclusive education to a special education subsystem has to be questioned and destabilized if we are to acheive transformative change based on a human rights approach to disability and difference (Liasidou, 2007). Critical and action oriented approaches to greater inclusive education policy and practice (Lingard and Mills, 2007) should be constructively combined in order to challenge the conceptual and pragmatic vestiges of special education status quo. A key element within this process is to recognize the emancipatory potentials of pedagogy, which can be used both as a practical and conceptual tool (critical pedagogy) for transformative change (see Chapter 2).

Defining inclusion: a semantic chameleon

Emanating from the social model of disability (Oliver, 1990), which puts the emphasis on disabling social barriers rather than individual deficits, inclusive education refers to the restructuring of social and, by implication, educational settings in order to meet the needs of all learners irrespective of their diverse biographical, developmental and learning trajectories. Inclusive education constitutes a radical paradigm shift and by no means should be considered as a linear progression from a special educational needs discourse. This said, inclusive education

> [S]hould never be a default vocabulary for Special Educational Needs. The moment we allow inclusive education to be special education for new times is the moment

we submit to collective indifference. . . . Inclusive education is code for educational reform at all levels. A new social imagination and congruent vocabulary is required that delivers us from the fortification of outdated traditions and practices of schooling. (Slee, 2011: 121–2)

Arguably, inclusion constitutes a response to the flawed ways in which the education of disabled students has been so far predicated, as it emanates from new theorizations of disability, whereby disability is not solely attributed to individual deficits. Rather, it is predominantly attributed to material and ideological disabling barriers that undermine the social, intellectual and emotional development of certain individuals. Within an inclusive context, children's atypical and diverse developmental trajectories are recognized and valued through a positive appreciation of difference for a socially just and fair society.

Nevertheless, despite its indisputable moral and ethical standing, the rhetoric advocating the realization of inclusion has been vociferously contested and characterized as a utopian pursuit (Croll and Moses, 2000) or a 'passionate intuition' (Pirrie and Head, 2007), while other analysts have pointed out the necessity to promote 'responsible inclusion' (Vaughan and Schumm, 1995).

Inclusion is a highly elusive notion whose interpretation, as well as implementation, are contingent on a vast array of discursive dynamics that give rise to varied and contradictory discourses, the latter defined as being the material effects of language-use, which constitute a coherent ensemble of ideas/regimes that exert social control by 'rendering some things common sense and other things nonsensical' (Youdell, 2006: 36). These discourses have according to Armstrong (1999: 76):

Multiple meanings, used by different people in different contexts, and are commonly used in ways which mask the attitudes, social structures and processes which produce and sustain exclusions.

The ideological melange underpinning inclusion is extremely diverse, nebulous and occasionally contradictory, something that is subsequently reconfigured and regenerated through the social and institutional arrangements that purport to promote the realization of an inclusive discourse. As Graham and Slee (2008b: 83) aptly put it, inclusion is 'troubled by the multiplicity of meanings that lurk within the discourses that surround and carry it'. It is not surprising then that some commentators talk about inclusion in the plural in order to denote its multiple facets and perspectives (Dyson, 1999).

Different people implicated in the debates around inclusion, as well as in the processes of policy formulation and implementation, have different understandings of inclusion and special educational needs. The field has been dominated by different theoretical camps holding diverse verdicts as to the feasibility of inclusion and its effectiveness to meet diverse needs. Quoting Clough and Corbett (2000: 6), '"Inclusion" is not a single *movement*; it is made up of many strong currents of belief, many different local struggles and a myriad of practices'. In a similar vein, Slee (2006: 111) suggests that: 'The theoretical and pragmatic imprecision of this thing we, and it is a very broad we, call inclusive education has permitted all manner of thinking, discourse and activity to pass of as inclusive'. The above statements denote the variegated nature of ideologically, culturally and historically grounded dynamics that bring to bear a prodigious impact on the ways in which inclusive education is conceptualized and acted upon.

The debates attract a disciplinarily heterogeneous group of people, who attempt to theorize inclusion according to their perceived optimal ways in which the latter can effectively meet learner diversity. Various models of inclusion are suggested and theorized in alignment with the ways in which difference is conceptualized and envisaged to be dealt with in mainstream schools (Booth and Ainscow, 1998; Rustemier, 2002; Farrell, 2009). In parallel with the debates around the social model of disability and the ways in which it can sufficiently explicate disability (Corker and French, 2001; Thomas, 2004), the debates have subsequently revolved around the different interpretations of inclusion, and the optimal educational arrangements that can effectively meet the needs of students designated as having special educational needs (Norwich, 2008a).

For instance, arguments in relation to inclusion revolve around its effectiveness, as well as its limitations, in meeting the individual needs of all students, and in particular, of those students with atypical developmental trajectories in terms of ability and attainment. The field has been an ongoing theoretical battlefield fraught with diverse perspectives and insights ranging from enthusiastic proclamations (e.g Stainback and Stainback, 1992; Thomas, 1997; Ainscow, 1997), to pessimistic and sceptical commentaries, as well as serious contemplations regarding the feasibility of inclusion as a means to providing the optimal learning environment for all students (Funch and Funch, 1994; Kauffman, 1995; Low, 1997; O'Brien, 2001; Farrell 2009).

The contentious nature of inclusion and Special Educational Needs (SEN) has been recently reinforced in the United Kingdom by Baroness Warnock's (2005, 2010) assertions regarding the position and future of segregated special provision whereby the author characterizes inclusion as a dangerous legacy.

While denouncing pessimistic and unsubstantiated allusions about the utopian nature of inclusion, by no means is it suggested that inclusion is an easy and uncontested pursuit. Inclusion is a complex concept embedded in what Norwich (2010: 93) calls 'a plural values framework' whereby contradictory existing and emerging values are juxtaposed, repositioned, contested and negotiated. The interactionist values framework, and the tensions accrued, need to be thoroughly explored and understood if we are to go beyond unilateral and deficit-oriented understanding of special educational needs that prevent us from developing and fostering an inclusive framework in meeting students' capabilities and needs.

Inclusion has been debated and contested to such a great extent that it has been occasionally diluted to an empty linguistic construct (Benjamin, 2002a). As Armstrong et al. (2010: 29) write: 'The reality is not simply that inclusion means different things to different people, but rather that inclusion may end up meaning everything and nothing at the same time.' This said, in attempting to demystify and disentangle the conceptual complexity and semantic plurality of inclusion, it is important to theorize some of the ways in which inclusion has been conceptualized, theorized and enacted. This chapter will be given over to exploring the multiplicity of meanings ascribed to inclusion. These meanings are diverse and contradictory, as well as historically and contextually rooted.

Reflective Exercise

What does inclusion mean to you?

Inclusive education and the question of change

Notwithstanding their occasional terminological fusion, inclusion is inherently different from integration as the two notions emanate from different conceptual antecedents and pedagogical discourses. While integration denotes a normalizing process that is primarily concerned with the relocation of disabled students in unchanged, assimilationist and monolithic educational systems (Thomas, 1997), inclusion presupposes the radical organizational, curricular and pedagogical change of schools, in order to respond to learner diversity (Booth and Ainscow, 2000; Mittler, 2000). In many instances, due to misconception and ideological confusion, inclusive education is perceived and acted upon as 'integration' and, hence, as a sub-system of special education within which several disguised forms of marginalization, discrimination and exclusion are operating.

Educational change is at the core of the struggles towards greater inclusion and, therefore, all the parameters, those either facilitating or undermining change, should be critically examined and analysed. Given the interactive framework of reciprocal relations and consequential effects, inclusion rejects the assimilationist view of integration, whereby the focus has been on the normalization of disabled people, and advocates instead a rights-discourse approach (Barton, 1993; Kenworthy and Whittaker, 2000; Rioux, 2002), characterized by 'a zero tolerance attitude to all forms of exclusion' (Barton, 2008a, xvii).

Inclusion does not seek to normalize allegedly 'defective' individuals, but seeks to subvert exclusionary social conditions and disabling educational practices, which oppress and subjugate disabled students by violating their basic human rights and undermining their human subject positions. The apposite characterization of 'maindumping' (Stainback and Stainback, 1992) – a metaphor used in order to describe the uncritical placement of disabled students in unprepared mainstream schools and classrooms – has been attributed to the abortive attempts to integrate certain groups of students in unchanged and monolithic mainstream schools. These uncritical integrative attempts have been solely aimed at the normalization of presumed 'defective' and 'abnormal' individuals in order to respond to the existing institutional and educational structures and expectations. The 'impaired self' has been scrutinized and forced to adapt to the existing institutional arrangements of mainstream schooling, along with the disciplinary practices inherent in it, without attempting to challenge the educational status quo (Foucault, 1977a).

Inclusion requires educational systems to be radically restructured so as to provide quality education for all students, especially the most vulnerable ones, irrespective of their individual characteristics and diverse biographical and developmental trajectories. That said, inclusion constitutes the response to the oppressive and unidimensional ways in which the education of disabled students has been so far predicated, as it emanates from a new theorization of disability, whereby disability is not solely attributed to individual deficits. Rather, it is predominantly attributed to environmental and ideological disabling barriers and oppressive institutional and ideological regimes. The individualistic gaze and the paraphernalia of its normalizing practices, centred upon singling out presumed defective individuals, are superseded by an institutional gaze aimed at initiating educational change and promoting sustainable school development (Panther, 2007; Eckins and Grimes, 2009).

Norwich (2010: 86) places some of the problems, dilemmas and possibilities with regard to inclusive education within the context of a 'transformed educational system'. Arguably, the concept of special educational needs is to a greater extent the result of an inadequate general educational system that significantly fails to cater to learner diversity. Special educational needs are thus used 'as a euphemism for failure' (Barton, 1996: 5) and as a way to justify schools' failure in accommodating the needs and abilities of a great percentage of the school population. Understandably, attempts to implement inclusion without pursuing a radical system change are likely to be either short-term or may fail altogether resulting in what might be called an 'inclusion backlash' (Dyson, 2001). Criticism with regard to inclusion in terms of its feasibility should recognize the fact that inclusion entails a revolutionary system change (Ainscow, 2005).

Given the multidimensional and highly complicated character of educational change, educational restructuring attempts should be directed towards a polymorphous and reciprocally related network incorporating a vast array of macro and micro dynamics (Power, 1992), some of which might be quite impermeable to change. The co-existence and convergence of certain micropolitical and structural factors occasionally consolidate and reinforce the special education status quo as they become naturalized and institutionally sacred (Liasidou, 2007).

Unless educational change is seriously concerned with questioning the status quo, inclusion will continue to be jeopardized and reduced to a special education subsystem. The struggles for inclusion (Vlachou, 1997) presuppose self-awareness, and necessitate an informed and serious recognition of the necessity to proceed to radical and fundamental educational and social restructuring. This venture entails reflexivity and critical engagement with the complexity of issues at hand, with a view to mobilizing transformative change. Towards this end, practitioners and researchers need to be willing to get actively involved in the process of change and become aware of their own significant contribution to the process of change (Barton, 2008a).

Notwithstanding the plethora of discursive and pragmatic impediments undermining transformative change, it is nevertheless a feasible pursuit when there is firm and unequivocal institutional, political and ideological convergence towards this end. As Oliver as early as in 1995 pointed out:

> Such has been the extent of this failure that nothing short of a complete deconstruction of the whole enterprise of Special Education will suffice . . . nothing short of a radical deconstruction of special education and the reconstruction of education in totality will be enough, even if the journey takes us another hundred years . . . (Oliver, 1995: 35, cited in Thomas and Vaughan, 2004: 112–13)

The following sections are given over to the different interpretations and perspectives on inclusion, along with the ways in which they are interlinked with and emanating from the wider socio-political and historical dynamics. A robust understanding of the notion of inclusion necessitates forging links and establishing consequential explanations with regard to the ways in which the different perspectives on inclusion are reciprocally interrelated with the wider socio-political system. The analysis of these interrelations and consequential effects can potentially bring to the surface the varied nature of dynamics that give rise to and affect the different discourses underpinning inclusion.

Reflective Exercise

What aspects of educational change are prioritized by inclusion?
What does change mean within your context of practice?

Perspectives on inclusion

Inclusion as a human rights issue

The realization of an inclusive discourse represents an ideological and rhetorical shift, and thereby policies and practices that relegate disabled students to the margins of educational and social domains are categorically denounced. Inclusion emerges from an entirely different knowledge base, where diversity is perceived as being the norm and considered as a positive and enriching experience. Slee (2011: 14) has argued that inclusive education 'offers an audacious challenge to the attachment of ascending and descending values to different people'.

Given the host of dynamics impinging on inclusive education policy constitution and dissemination, any definitions of inclusion are inadequate unless conjured up against the backdrop of a human rights approach to disability and difference. The inclusion of disabled students in mainstream schools should be primarily a commitment to reinstate their human rights as equally valued members of society. By no means should inclusive education be considered as a sacrifice or a privilege to be 'earned' (Rioux, 2002: 214). Rather, inclusion should be unambiguously regarded as a matter of entitlement and as an attempt to develop 'a vision of democracy through difference', where disabled people realize 'their social, political and civil rights of citizenship' (Barton, 1997: 235). Moreover, the concept of inclusion is part of the wider concern for equity and social justice, based on a human rights approach to social relations, with a view to combating sources of disadvantage and marginalization resulting from, and giving rise to, negative connotations of difference and diversity.

Inclusive education, conjured up against an ethics and rights discourse, is defined as being 'a project of cultural politics, as part of the politics of identity, difference and representation (Young, 1990; Fraser, 1995) as they are played out in the social relations of schooling' (Slee, 2001a: 386). The ultimate aim is to re-instate the eroded subject positions and subjugated identities of marginalized and stigmatized groups of students.

Issues of exclusion, marginalization and oppression have been addressed and challenged through a human rights approach to difference and diversity (Barton and Armstrong, 2007) aimed at subverting the 'Othering' (denoting a condescending perspective with regard to 'others' who are different from 'us') and inferior images attributed to certain individuals, on the basis of their presumed abnormality with regard to a monodimensional and insular conceptions of normalcy (Tremain, 2005). The notion of normalcy is used as a heuristic device in order to calibrate presumed deviations from arbitrarily construed notions of normality on the basis of ability, gender, ethnicity and socio-economic background.

Inclusion, in this respect, becomes a struggle against overt and covert processes of exclusion and marginalization, affecting great masses of people, especially the most vulnerable ones. It is about subverting imposition, domination and giving scope for nurturing acceptance, tolerance, respect and celebration of difference (Barton, 1997). Difference is now, according to Barton (1997: 235) 'to be viewed as a challenge, a means of generating change and encouragement for people to question unfounded generalizations, prejudice and discrimination'. Segregating practices are nothing but a violation of human rights since disabled children are treated differently from their peers and are refused access to mainstream education.

The Centre for Studies in Inclusive Education regards 'full inclusion' as a human rights issue and advocates the abolition of segregated (special) schooling, while others hold that a special education school system has no place within a right-based framework (Cigman, 2006). Quoting Kenworty and Whittaker (2000: 222):

> Ending the segregation of children is above all, a human rights objective . . . The conviction must be that segregated education is a damaging and archaic practice, incompatible with a civilised society.

Towards this end, it is crucial that the philosophical tenets of inclusion should be clarified and differentiated from persistent orthodoxies of the past, which have so far masked and disguised assumptions inimical to inclusion. The traditional linkage of inclusion with special education should be jettisoned, while the linkage of inclusion with human rights should be urgently forged as the first critical step towards emancipatory change (Barton, 2005), for more just and equitable educational and social systems for all. By no means should inclusive education leave any room for complacency when its tenets are at stake.

The aim should be to meet learner diversity, as a part of a human rights approach discourse (Starkey, 1991), where differences are celebrated, individual needs are recognized, and all forms of oppression are removed. The conceptualization of the historically, socially and culturally contingent nature of inclusion can potentially challenge to a significant extent iniquitous ideological predispositions, fears and biases that have so far diluted the road towards emancipatory change through the reinstatement and enhancement of human rights for all.

As Barton and Armstrong (2007: 6) write,

> For us inclusive education is not an end in itself, but a means to an end. It is about contributing to the realisation of an inclusive society with a demand for a rights approach as a central component of policy-making. Thus the question is fundamentally about issues of human rights, equity, social justice and the struggle for

a non-discriminatory society. These principles are at the heart of inclusive educational policy and practice.

Exemplified as a human rights and moral issue, segregated provision is regarded as a form of institutional discrimination (Rustemier, 2002b) while the attempts towards inclusion are defined, for instance, on par with the attempts to abolish slavery. The parallel sets out a strong rationale for inclusion and counteracts, to a great extent, criticisms over the lack of unequivocal empirical evidence supporting inclusion. As the following quote suggests:

> Unfortunately, science cannot offer a positive or negative answer to mainstreaming . . . At the time of the American Civil War, should Abraham Lincoln have asked to see the scientific evidence on the benefits of ending slavery? Should he have consulted 'the expert', perhaps a sociologist, an economist, a political scientist? Of course not . . . Slavery is not now and was not then an issue of science. It is a moral issue. (Bilken, 1985: 16, cited in Thomaz et al., 2009: 558)

The above quote is very powerful in documenting the reasons as to why inclusion should constitute an unambiguous pursuit on the basis of a human rights approach to disability and difference. This position is also strongly advocated by disabled people and their organizations (Ainscow and Cesar, 2006). Inclusion in this respect is conceptualized as being essentially an attempt to restructure current schooling so as to celebrate differences and respond to students' diversity in socially just and democratic ways. In this respect,

> Advocates of inclusive education predicate their philosophy on arguments of social justice and ideals of the Just and Good Society. Their aim is that education becomes a transformative and positive experience for all as opposed to an exclusionary process, where commitments to equality and diversity are not just respected ideas but enacted practices. (Gibson and Haynes, 2009: 1)

The Salamanca Statement made clear, as early as 1994, the obligation of nation states to protect and enhance the rights of disabled students. The declaration, which was signed by delegates representing 92 governments and 25 international organizations, proclaims the fundamental right of every child to access inclusive mainstream schools. It clearly states: 'Inclusion and participation are essential to human dignity and to the enjoyment and exercise of human rights' (UNESCO, 1994: 61). In 2006 UNESCO launched a Human

Rights Action Plan which promotes human rights through education and in education. In particular it is suggested that:

> Human rights education promotes a holistic, rights-based approach that includes both 'human rights through education', ensuring that all the components and processes of education – including curricula, materials, methods and training – are conducive to the learning of human rights, and 'human rights in education', ensuring that the human rights of all members of the school community are respected (UNESCO, 2006: 8)

Another significant development with regard to a human rights approach to disability and difference was the enforcement of the United Nations Convention on the Rights of Persons with Disabilities on 3 May 2008. The convention recognizes the relative nature of disability, which is the result of the interaction of a person's impairment with institutional and environmental barriers that prohibit 'their full and effective participation in society on an equal basis with others' (United Nations, 2008: 1). The focus on students' 'needs' should therefore be diverted to their 'need' to be viewed as equal and valuable human beings entitled to socially just and equal educational opportunities in their local mainstream schools. The notion of 'needs' deflects attention from the necessity to promote policies and practices imbued by the discourse of rights and equal opportunities (Roaf and Bines, 1989).

Hence, the notions of human rights and inclusion should be understood as being inexorably linked, as the recognition of disabled students' human rights should be at the heart of the struggles towards the realization of inclusion. In this respect, the debates around inclusion should concentrate on the necessity to forge and explicate a clear link between human rights and inclusion. This can be achieved by acquiring a meaningful understanding of a human rights approach and its implications for inclusive education policy and practice. As Kenworthy and Whittaker (2000: 223) argue:

> Those who promote 'inclusive education' must be convinced of the human rights foundation and be prepared to assert it plainly and publicly if there is to be genuine progress toward equality for all children and their families. By failing to assert the right of the individual child we undermine the credibility of the campaign for the human rights of all children. We cannot hide behind the 'illusion of choice'.

Unless this interconnection is forged, the individualistic gaze will continue to place disabled individuals in inferior subject positions. If we are to destabilize and challenge the powerful circle that leads to the oppression and disparagement of disabled people, questions like the following should constitute the focal point of our critical inquiry:

- What is a human rights approach to disability?
- What actions are necessary in order to facilitate a human rights approach to disability?
- How, why and on what basis are certain groups of people constructed as 'different'?
- How can a human rights approach be applied in education policy and practice?

Dyson (1999) discusses the existence of two discourses underpinning the attempts towards greater inclusive policy and practice. One of the discourses is the discourse of rights and ethics that centres upon the rights of disabled students, along with the ways in which their rights can be met within schools on an equal and non-discriminatory basis. The second discourse, articulated by Dyson, is the efficacy discourse that is concerned with the parameters of schooling that can potentially enhance inclusion. Similarly, Mitchell (2008) has distilled a vast array of studies that provide substantial evidence supporting the effectiveness of certain whole-school and classroom practices that can potentially enhance inclusion. The effectiveness discourse and the school effectiveness movement (Ainscow, 2005b; Dyson, 1999), however, are void and meaningless unless placed within and discussed against the context of the ethics and rights discourse. The cross-fertilization and synergetic relationship between both discourses are crucial prerequisites in the attempts to challenge the special education status quo.

Inclusion cannot be achieved unless there is a synergetic relation between institutional and ideological dynamics, between pragmatic and critical approaches to policy and practice. Critical and action oriented approaches (Lingard and Mills, 2007), as well as an interdisciplinary analytical framework, should be constructively combined in order to challenge the conceptual and pragmatic paraphernalia of the special education status quo, while exploring the possibilities of fostering more inclusive forms of provision without swiftly and uncritically 'closing down to a separatist resolution' (Norwich, 2010: 74). Any kind of unilateral analyses of the issues at stake is incomplete and does not do any justice to the sheer complexity of issues, tensions and dilemmas pertaining to the notions of inclusion, disability and special educational needs (Barton, 1996, 1998a, 1998b, 2003; Corker and Shakespeare, 2002a).

We should also bear in mind that the notion of human rights can be looked at from different perspectives (e.g., whose rights and under what conditions), something that has profound implications for the ways in which inclusion is theorized and acted upon. While inclusion as a human rights entitlement holds an unambiguous moral ground, this perspective is, nevertheless, contested. This is because mainstream placements for certain individuals can arguably undermine their right to quality education, as well as other children's human rights and educational entitlements (Warnock, 2010). Inclusion is conceptualized in terms of students' participation in common enterprises of learning that can be either in special or mainstream settings. It is suggested (e.g., Warnock, 2010, 2005; Farrell, 2009) that what is more important is the right of children to learning, regardless of where learning might take place, a position that will be further explored in the following section. The notion of human rights is also conceptualized in terms of safeguarding non-disabled children's rights and educational entitlements. The latter point holds especially true when including students designated as having social, emotional and behavioural difficulties, whose behaviour might be challenging and disruptive.

Thus, the conceptualization of inclusion as a matter of human rights raises the questions of whose rights and under what conditions. The ambivalence of a human rights perspective with regard to educational placement is reflected for instance in the anti-discriminatory educational legislation currently enforced in England and Wales. The 2001 Special Educational Needs and Disability Act (HMSO, 2001) pronounces discrimination against disabled people unlawful in conditional terms. In spite of the fact that the Act stipulates that a child with Special Educational Needs must be educated in a mainstream school , this is contingent on whether the presence of the child affects adversely the provision of efficient education for other children.

Reflective Exercise

Why is inclusive education a human rights issue?

Inclusion as a means to social cohesion and economic advancement

Occasionally, inclusive education is equated with the notion of social inclusion, which is concerned with wider issues pertaining to the social exclusion and marginalization of certain vulnerable groups prone to exclusionary pressures and discriminatory practices. Within educational contexts the notion of social inclusion has referred to high risk of exclusion groups of students like female students who become pregnant or have babies, looked after children and travellers. However, in most cases the social inclusion agenda is narrowly concerned with students in danger of exclusion due to their 'behaviour' (Ainscow and Miles, 2008).

The notion of social inclusion also has some other connotations aligned with the standards agenda (Dyson, 2001, 2005; Roulstone and Prideaux, 2008). In order to understand the ways in which this link is conceptualized, it is important to explore the complex relationship between inclusive education policymaking, politics and the economy. As Barton (1987: 132) writes, '... part of the challenges facing those concerned with the question of inclusion involves making connections between educational ideologies, policies and practices and the wider social and economic conditions and relations of a given society.'

For instance, currently policies on inclusive education are significantly informed by the wider neo-liberal constructions of inclusion driven by economic imperatives and social cohesion concerns, the aim being to render hitherto unproductive groups of individuals more productive, so as to contribute to the highly demanding and competitive workforce of the twenty first century (Taylor, 2004; Dyson, 2005). Globalization instigates the necessity to ensure the development of a skilled and versatile workforce capable of contributing to a nation state's competitiveness in the global economy. As Ball (2009: 11) writes: 'Within policy, education is now regarded primarily from an economic point of view.'

The notion of social inclusion is thus used as a means to maximize the economic and social usefulness of 'docile bodies' (Foucault, 1979: 138), thereby ignoring the cultural politics of inclusion and special educational needs (Armstrong, 2005). Hence, while the inclusion agenda predicated on a human rights approach to disability and difference, focuses on students' presence and participation in mainstream schools, social inclusion focuses more on educational outcomes and on the re-engagement of disaffected groups with learning, irrespective of educational placement (Dyson, 2001, 2005). The educational tenets of social inclusion revolve around the necessity to create the optimal learning environment capable of meeting learners' diverse needs irrespective of educational placement. 'Inclusivity' in this respect is not perceived as being associated with the notion of belonging and participation in mainstream local educational settings. Rather, the former is perceived in relation to its potential to re-engage disaffected learners in the learning process, in order to achieve educational excellence that is solely measured against examination results and league table rankings. At a policy level, segregated placements are represented as being part of the 'inclusion' agenda in terms of learning and learner participation (Dyson, 2005; Lloyd, 2008) thereby suggesting that special schools might be as inclusive as mainstream schools. These new forms of neo-liberal constructions of inclusion consolidate and perpetuate the notion of 'special educational needs' and the paraphernalia of deficit oriented approaches of cure and remedy associated with it.

The neo-liberal constructions of inclusion have given rise to the contradictory character of inclusive education policy documents. Recent policy documents are replete with contradictions and ambiguities (Taylor, 2004; Lloyd, 2008; Liasidou, 2008b, 2011). On the one hand inclusion in mainstream settings is presented as a matter of human rights, while on the other hand segregated placements are presented as being concerned with learners' rights to learn (Farrell, 2009). This is also related to contradictory considerations over the aims of education. We should bear in mind that inclusive education is about values and principles; it is about the kind of education we want and the kind of education we value and prioritize. From a human rights perspective it is asserted that 'Inclusive education is based on the right of all learners to a quality education that meets basic learning needs and enriches lives' (UNESCO, 2009: 1). Nevertheless, very often education policy and practice concentrate on the products of learning (e.g., DCSF, 2009b) rather than the process of learning, with the former measured against exam results and monodimensional fabrications of successful schools (Ball, 2001). Ball (2003, 2004, 2009) talks about the 'terrors of perfomativity' whereby teachers are required to:

> produce measurable and 'improving' outputs and performances . . . Increasingly, we choose and judge our actions and they are judged by others on the basis of their contribution to organizational performance, rendered in terms of measurable outputs. Beliefs are no longer important – it is output that counts. (Ball 2003: 222)

Under these circumstances, disabled students are regarded as being a major threat to school's 'perfomativity' and consequent league table positioning, thereby leading to their marginalization and exclusion from mainstream settings. For instance, Barton and Armstrong (2007: 7) raise concerns about current policy initiatives in the United Kingdom allegedly intended to enhance educational 'choice and personalization', that evasively, albeit poignantly, exclude and marginalize certain pupils and counteract ambitions for 'an open, equitable and democratic system of education'. The notions of 'choice' aligned with the standards agenda, along with the proliferation of 'pull out' educational programmes intended for individuals with presumed individual and social pathologies are at the fore, thereby giving rise to new forms of segregation within mainstream settings.

While exploring issues of equity and leadership, Ross and Berger (2009, p. 470) point to the necessity to 'discourage strategies that involve "gaming" the accountability system'. Gaming consists of a number of practices deployed by schools in order to discreetly marginalize and exclude certain students and prevent them from adding negative value to a school's performance indicators in relation to minimizing achievement gaps attributable to race, culture, language, ability and gender (Graham and Jahnukainen, 2011; Ross and Berger, 2009). Practices of 'gaming' have also a pervasive role in adopting particular teaching strategies and assessment procedures that are more concerned with the outcomes of high stakes assessments rather than with an inclusive education reform agenda (Sindelar et al., 2006). Within this context, success is constructed in mono-dimensional ways (Benjamin, 2002b) and there is evidence of 'uneven quality of curriculum provision beyond literacy and numeracy' (Alexander, 2009: 3).

The *Rose Report* (DCSF, 2009c) and the *Cambridge Review* (Alexander, 2009) in the United Kingsom point to the necessity to achieve a better curriculum balance with regard to relevance, breadth and creativity. It is 'teaching and not testing' (Alexander, 2009: 4) that can potentially enhance educational standards:

> While the government's childhood agenda is applauded, its standards agenda is viewed less favourably – not from opposition to standards and accountability but because of the educational damage the apparatus of targets, testing, performance tables, national strategies and inspection is perceived to have caused for questionable returns. (Alexander, 2009: 2)

The contradictory nature of policy in the United Kingdom can be explained through for instance, Anthony Giddens' (1998) theorizations of 'Third way' politics attempt to bring together social democratic and free market ideals in education (Dyson, 2005; Ball, 2009). Also, the contradictory official policy landscape can be explained through the notion of 'symbolic policy' whereby some policies are introduced for electoral advantage rather than in order to address a real problem (Brehony, 2005).

For instance, in order to respond to criticisms regarding the subordination of a child centred education to economic imperatives, the UK Government introduced some policy documents, which put a pronounced emphasis on the processes of learning and the need to respond to individual needs and abilities (Brehony, 2005). This is reflected in DfES (2003a) policy document on Enjoyment and Achievement which suggests that the notion of education involves more than attainment. The same line of thought is adopted in the National Strategy; Social and Emotional Aspects of Learning (DfES, 2007) that puts an emphasis on the processes of learning and the need to enable students to develop positive behaviour towards learning as a means for self-fulfilment. The symbolic value of the above policies was confirmed by the White Paper (DCSF, 2009b) 'Your child, Your schools, Our future', which, in stark contrast to the above policy documents adopts a utilitarian approach to education.

In much the same way, Taylor (2004) documents the ways in which Educational Policies in Queensland, Australia are characterized by 'discursive multiplicity' as they attempt to align concerns for equity and social justice with neo-liberal constructions of educational excellence. In much the same way, Marshall and Patterson (2002), discuss the contradictory and ambivalent special education reform agenda in the United States of America, whereby 'Policies, programs, reforms, political pressures and legal mandates push in different directions and thus confuse and confound educators' (Marshall and Patterson, 2002: 351).

Inclusion as a special educational subsystem

The reduction of inclusive education to a special education artefact has to be interrogated and challenged if we are to achieve transformative change based on a human rights approach to disability and special educational needs. Notwithstanding ample rhetoric around inclusion, segregated and assimilationist practices are still thriving (Barton and Armstrong, 2007;

Graham and Jahnukainen, 2011). These practices reflect the reductionist and hence ambivalent character of current policy initiatives pertaining to inclusive education. An example is the UK Government's strategy for SEN (DfES, 2004), which contradicts itself in very blatant ways as it is concerned both with the issue of inclusion and the need to maintain and develop special schools. At the same time, the policy document is riddled with references to compensatory models of support and individual pathology perspectives, thereby placing the gaze on children's presumed 'deficits'. Thus, rather than concentrating on removing barriers to learning endemic to the curriculum, the assessment regimes and institutional conditions of current schooling, the document is concerned with providing early intervention and compensatory measures of support (Lloyd, 2008). Under the siege of the neo-liberal standards agenda and the subsequent utilitarian ethos of modern schooling, the blame is squarely placed on individual students and their presumed individual and family pathology, thereby finding recourse to traditional special educational practices.

Proponents of the twin track system (Warnock 2005, 2010) denounce inclusion on the grounds that is axiomatically difficult, if not impossible, to meet a wide spectrum of abilities within a single educational setting. More recent policy initiatives in the United Kingdom go so far as to stipulate the necessity to 'remove the bias towards inclusion' (DfE, 2011: 17). The legacy of special schools is presented as a means to providing optimal educational alternatives to groups of students who allegedly might not benefit from mainstream provision (Low, 1997; Croll and Moses, 2000; Warnock 2010). Thus concerns for inclusion in terms of educating all students under 'the same roof' are superseded by a concern for providing 'a common enterprise of learning' irrespective of educational placement, without considering the possibility of perhaps other 'hybrid' and versatile educational alternatives (Norwich, 2010: 82).

Inevitably, such assumptions render the scope of inclusion limited and, hence, ineffective for certain groups of individuals who do not fall within the remit of so-called 'normal' and 'conventionally educable' student population. Special education is regarded as being a legitimate alternative to meeting the needs of certain individuals with profound and complex needs, while leaving intact the normal operation of mainstream schooling. At the same time, the notions of 'choice' and 'voice' figure prominently in the current debates around inclusion, with particular reference to certain groups and individuals who might prefer alternative educational placements. Armstrong et al. (2010)

cite the example of the Deaf community whose interpretation of inclusion is constricted to the inclusion of its members to 'the Deaf community', the latter being defined as a linguistic minority in need of specialist educational provision.

The question however, as to whether these alternative placements can be characterized as being inclusive remains. Norwich (2010: 101) while commenting on the ambivalent current UK policy with regard to inclusion poses the following questions:

- If children with disabilities spend part of their time outside ordinary classrooms, is that consistent with inclusion?
- And if it is, how much separation is consistent with inclusion?
- Are part-time placements in off-site settings for appropriate and time-limited learning compatible with inclusion?
- The point is that once some degree of 'withdrawal' from the general system is accepted, then this raises the question of how far to go and when does this become exclusion?

Along similar lines, Graham and Sweller (2011: 2) pose the following questions:

- If we do not embrace full inclusion, where do we draw the line?
- Who should be included and who should not?
- Where does 'severe' end and 'profound' begin?
- Are some children with disabilities less welcome in their local school than others?
- Who decides?

In trying to challenge certain conceptualizations of inclusion, it is important to analyse the ways in which the notion of difference has been constructed as learning and behaviour problems in schools and has been mobilized as a legitimate mechanism of managing and containing certain groups of children (Armstrong et al., 2010). Arguably, these 'alternative placements' are nothing but a legitimate mechanism of managing potentially 'troublesome' individuals who allegedly have nothing to contribute to the utilitarian ethos of modern schooling. Different kinds of human 'deviance' have been thus devised and gauged against an arbitrarily construed notion of normality (Graham, 2005) with a view to protecting the normal functioning of mainstream schooling.

Historically, the individualistic and deficit oriented influence of special educational thinking has concentrated on students' deficits and obscured external parameters, while the normalizing judgement has construed disabled students as 'abnormal' and 'deviant' who should be disciplined and brought to line, through an array of 'rationalized' technologies of power imposed on them. The dominant assumption has been, as Morton and Gibson (2003: 13) write, that the 'goal of the individual is to be fixed'. There has been little room for other considerations or alternative 'regimes of truth' (Foucault, 1984a) intended to expose and gauge the ways in which social, ideological, political and institutional dynamics have been complicit in the emergence and proliferation of disabling regimes. Societies create and perpetuate 'regimes of truth' that are (re)generated, disseminated and acted upon by dominant social institutions (e.g., schools, professionals, legislation), and have a pervasive impact on constructing and positioning social relations and human subjectivities.

The traditional interlinking of special education with the scientific and functional 'regimes of truth', has consolidated and perpetuated a deficit-based form of thinking, which distorted the political and contested nature of the field and, arguably, acted to the detriment of disabled children and their advocates. The influence of this form of thinking is still rife, albeit in more subtle and opaque ways, thereby impeding transformative change. Graham (2006), for instance, characterizes the contemporary phenomenon of ADHD (Attention Deficit Hyperactivity Disorder) as a 'symptom of the pathologies of schooling' whereby schooling is portrayed:

> as a site for disciplinary power via the 'ab-normalisation' of child behaviour (. . .) [Such an approach provides] . . .schools and teachers with an 'e/scape-goat' – an excuse for schooling failure in the form of the sick but somehow bad and therefore *punishable* child. (Graham, 2006: 2) (emphasis in the original)

It is occasionally assumed that individual intervention programmes and compensatory measures of support (Lloyd, 2008) can satisfactorily meet the needs of these children and enable them to 'catch up' with their peers. In this respect, the aim is according to Slee and Weiner (2001: 94) 'to support special needs [sic] students as they struggle to adapt to the demands of traditional schools and classrooms. . . . Inclusive education is a normaliing quest – it is an assimilationist imperative'.

Resource Units or Learning Support Units (LSUs) are a prime example of the resurgence of special education imperatives in mainstream settings (Liasidou, 2007; Graham and Sweller, 2011) as they constitute a subtle, albeit corrosive, exclusionary device within mainstream settings. Resource Units, or as euphemistically called 'inclusive units' are a conspicuous characteristic of many educational systems across the globe, whereby the notion of inclusion is reduced to assimilationist practices that bear no resemblance to the principles of an inclusive discourse. These units are starkly oriented to a segregating model, and seldom do they function as a transitional mode of education, aimed at facilitating the gradual inclusion of disabled children in mainstream classes.

The proliferation of remedial education practices in mainstream schools (Lloyd, 2008) create and consolidate negative connotations of difference, thereby leading to a 'denial of difference' and contributing to the devaluing and, hence, marginalization of students who are regarded as being different. Segregated remedial classes, allegedly aimed to enable certain individuals to 'catch up' with their peers, consolidate catastrophic 'normal' and 'abnormal' binaries and accentuate the 'othering' image imputed to certain individuals.

Resource Units are the technique by which the individual pathology perspectives increases 'to a maximum the visibility of those subjected' (Dreyfus and Rabinow, 1982: 192). The placement of disabled children in Resource Units increase their 'visibility' within mainstream settings as they constitute ' a centre toward which all gazes would be turned' (Foucault, 1977a: 173). The various SEN professionals provide individualistic sessions in these mini special schools, where the focus is squarely placed on children's perceived 'deficits'. In this way the 'individualistic gaze' singles out 'defective individuals' with presumed 'distorted' developmental and learning trajectories, thereby consolidating and perpetuating dichotomous perspectives of normality and abnormality (Slee, 2001a; Liasidou, 2008b).

For Foucault space is crucial in any exercise of power, and Resource Units constitute '. . . the spatial "nesting" of hierarchised surveillance . . . The principle was one of "embedding"' (Foucault, 1977a: 171–2). The 'embedding' of resource units in mainstream schools increase the level of surveillance exerted on disabled individuals, and resource units can be understood as part of the institutional central which in Foucault's (1977: 172) terms:

> Permit an internal articulated and detailed control to render visible those who are inside it; in more general terms an architecture that would operate to transform individuals; to act on those it shelters, to provide a hold on their conduct, to carry the effects of power right to them, to make possible to know them, to alter them.

Similar concerns can be raised in relation to the presence of teaching assistants in mainstream classrooms, whose role is usually constricted to the 'velcro model' of support, whereby they are 'virtually attached to the side of their students' (Fraser and Shields, 2010: 9) and expected to work with individual students on a one to one basis. In so doing, disabled students are isolated and socially marginalized from their peers, who assume that disabled children do not need their attention and friendship as they have the constant presence and attention of a teaching aide.

Notwithstanding the occasional innocuous and benevolent intentions of such approaches (Tomlinson, 1982; Ware, 2002), it is nevertheless suggested that practices which place the focus on children's differences, stigmatize, categorize, label and ultimately marginalize these groups of students. These approaches represent as Meijer, et al. (1997) put it a 'transplantation' of special education into mainstream settings thereby impeding the attempts towards radical educational reform disassociated from assimiliationist practices of the past.

In this respect, inclusive education policy imperatives are occasionally characterized by reductionism, in the sense that inclusion is constricted to the traditional special educational framework and used as a euphemism for exclusion (Barton, 1998), which is rhetorically disguised and embellished in current schooling. This is what Slee (2007: 179) calls 'the assimilation imperative of neo-special educational rhetoric and practice', which reflects an obscure, ambiguous and essentially unchanged philosophical orientation. Understandably, this kind of assimilationist imperative 'often has little to do with establishing an inclusive curriculum, pedagogic practices or classroom organization to reconstruct schools'. Rather, it is usually a 'systematic approach to acquiring human resources to mind the disabled student' (Slee, 2007: 181).

Reductionist models of 'inclusion' are merely concerned with the placement of disabled students in unchanged and monolithic mainstream settings disregarding, however, the fact that these students are also entitled to receive quality education and become active and valuable members of mainstream learning communities. Based on the individual deficit model of pathology and difference, their placement in mainstream settings becomes an inherently assimilationist process, since disabled individuals are singled out as being negatively different through an array of normalizing special education practices and compensatory measures of support. The focus is on the categorization of certain students as having special educational needs due to their low attainment, behaviour or disability. Within this framework difference is considered as a 'euphemism for defect or for abnormality' (Corbett and Slee,

2000, p. 134) and students who cannot fit to the existing monodimensional school organization and culture are designated as students with special educational needs.

The above considerations also raise concerns over the validity of the language of special educational needs in the discussion about inclusion. It is important to critically question and ultimately challenge the language of special education, and the deficit-oriented constructs associated with it. The role of language is significant in exerting social control and creating naturalizing effects on practice (Fairclough, 2001) something that will be explored in more detail in Chapter 5. The authors of the *Index for Inclusion* –a document providing a comprehensive guidance in fostering greater inclusive policy and practice – Tony Booth and Mel Ainscow (2002) disavow the use of the language of special educational needs and focus on the notion of barriers to learning and participation instead.

An emphasis on exploring the role of language in exerting social control entails looking beyond the meaning of inclusive policies and deciphering the 'various rhetorical and metaphorical devices that are used to gloss over their contradictions, inconsistencies and silences' (Skrtic, 1991: 36). Put simply, the aim is to expose the impediments to inclusion which emanate from the 'individualistic gaze' placed upon students' alleged 'deficits', rather than on the disabling procedures, structures and mechanisms that subvert inclusion. Ultimately then it will be possible, as Slee (1997: 413) succinctly puts it, to 'interrogate the meaning of inclusion' and thereby the aims of inclusive education policies by exposing exclusion 'in all its forms, the language we use, the teaching methods we adopt, the curriculum we transmit and the relation we establish within our schools . . .' (Corbett and Slee, 2000: 134) (see also Chapter 5).

The proliferation of assimilationist models of support in mainstream schooling (Lloyd, 2008) disregard the intersections of class, race, ethnicity and culture in formulating debates and devising practices in order to accommodate learner's diverse needs and biographical realities. Consequently, concerns over the role of the school within the community (Mittler, 1999; DCSF, 2009a) and issues of school improvement both in organization and pedagogy (Mitchell, 2008; Ekins and Grimes, 2009) are marginalized and considered as unimportant. On the contrary, the essentialist perspective of a deficit-based discourse is adopted in order to cover the inadequacies of the school apparatus to provide quality education for all (Vlachou, 1997) and minimize failure among students.

Understandably, given the above considerations, it is imperative that the implicit and explicit connections of special and inclusive education are jettisoned. Exclusion is primarily the result of what we might call a conceptual misinterpretation of inclusion. Insofar as the notion of inclusion is contingent on an array of exclusionary ideological and institutional dynamics, it will never cease to constitute a rhetorical apparition thereby securing its 'ghostly presence' (Slee and Allan, 2001: 17) within all arenas of educational policymaking. Inclusive education should be conjured up as being another more descriptive name for effective and quality education for all. Failure to understand the tenets of an inclusive discourse is a failure to understand the needs of the vast majority of school population. Unless it is conceptually established and clarified that disabled students are entitled to be given the same chances as their peers are, inclusion will continue to be misinterpreted and jeopardized by the historical imperatives of special educational thinking, masqueraded under the banner of inclusion.

Reflective Exercise

In what ways is the notion of inclusion reduced to a special education subsystem?

Is it always possible to provide appropriate support in mainstream classrooms or is temporary/part-time removal from the mainstream classroom a better option in some cases?

Inclusion as education for all

Inclusion cannot be achieved unless it is thoroughly explored and understood as a highly political act and a political pursuit that necessitates a reflexive stance and critical enquiry into a profusion of discursive dynamics that give rise to exclusionary practices and mentalities. An enhanced understanding of the complex processes and multiple dynamics impinging upon inclusion may elucidate the reasons as to why inclusion has increasingly become a heated educational debate and a battlefield of diverse perspectives and insights.

Ainscow et al. (2006) distinguish between the 'narrow' and 'broad' definitions of inclusion. The former is concerned with specific groups of individuals, who share certain characteristics, with particular reference to children with special educational needs and/or disabilities. The broad definition of inclusion, on the other hand, is concerned with learner diversity and the ways in which schools can respond to this diversity. Learner diversity is portrayed as consisting of distinct groups of students: boys and girls, looked after children, children from minority ethnic, faith and linguistic groups, gifted and talented and so on. In this respect, special educational needs and disabilities are subsumed within the bandwagon of learner diversity, thereby raising concerns over the effectiveness of these broader definitions of inclusion to effectively meet children's needs. As Norwich (2002: 493) writes the effect of such an indiscriminate and all-encompassing approach 'could be to dissolve disability issues in education into a wider more amorphous inclusive education'. This proposition can be more lucidly articulated in terms of the tension between commonality and differentiation stances whereby the notion of inclusion is based on a complex and, perhaps for some people, mutually exclusive interrelation of the values of equality and common provision and respect for individual differences.

The above concerns mirror the 'dilemma of difference' (Norwich, 2008a; 2009) and the various ways in which 'difference' can be conceptualized and acted upon in educational settings. On the one hand, it is suggested that the recognition of difference runs the risk of 'labelling' and 'stigmatizing' some students, thereby contributing to their further exclusion from mainstream schools and societies. At the same time, there is a counterargument that failure to recognize difference runs the risk, through pedagogical homogeneity, of ironing out individual 'differences' thereby failing to address and provide for individual needs (Norwich, 2008a).

The debates around the 'dilemma of difference' alert us to the necessity of recognizing disabled students' differences, and hence difficulties, in order to adequately meet their individual educational needs. However, the recognition of difference, as already discussed, is not without repercussions, since it is usually ushered in by a plethora of stigmatizing practices and exclusionary techniques, which undermine attempts towards the realization of an inclusive discourse predicated on a human rights approach to disability. The paraphernalia of special educational thinking and practice are paradoxically reconfigured within mainstream settings, whereby disabled students are subjected to a host of exclusionary and discriminatory practices that create and accentuate the 'otherness' image imputed to them. As Graham and Slee (2008b: 92–3) contend in relation to the 'dilemma of difference':

> When we identify categories of children, whether we refer to children at risk or children with a disability . . . , we not only make difference *visible* but work to maintain power imbalances and structural inequity by reifying *unnamed* attributes that carry social, political and cultural currency. (emphasis in the original)

The categorization of disabled and non-disabled children acts as a discourse of power and as 'a mechanism for spatialising procedures which sort people in different sites' (Armstrong, 2002: 450). The resolution of this dilemma lies in the identification of the optimal intersection or balance of diverse dynamics in order to facilitate inclusion. The intersection though, is precarious as it is spatially, culturally and socially contingent. The answer to the dilemma of difference is thus difficult to pinpoint or articulate. As Norwich (2010: 104) suggests while attempting to provide some tentative resolutions with regard to the dilemma of difference,

> The implication of the above analyses is that policy decisions involve striking some balance between commonality and differentiation stances in relation to various important dimensions of provision. Also, commonality and differentiation aspects of policies and practices cannot be detached from each other; the more commonality oriented policies still have some differentiation aspects and vice versa. This means furthermore that there are continuing risks of the negative consequences of differentiation and commonality stances. This means that there is no place for oversimplified splits or dichotomies too often found in debates over inclusion and should mean the avoidance of the futile pursuit of ideological purity.

At the same time the mere existence of this dilemma raises serious questions as to who defines 'difference' and what it means. Challenging normative assumptions of what deviates from conventional notions of bodily and intellectual ability, entails questions like 'When does difference count, under what conditions, in what ways, and for what reasons?' (Artiles, 1998: 32). That said, an arbitrary notion of normality, against which difference is construed and theorized, comes into play. As Dyson and Howes (2009: 57) put it:

> It is still the case that different resolutions [in relation to the dilemma of difference] embody different understandings of difference and different value positions. They originate from, embody and serve to reproduce particular socio-political positions and therefore tend to favour some interests over others.

That said, the 'dilemma of difference' should be regarded as a 'game of truth' (Graham, 2005: 5) that necessitates a critical engagement with the ways in which this

> . . . particular game might be played . . . [so as to].interrogate mechanisms that one could argue are complicit in the attribution of names, designation of subjects and assignment of spaces within and of the field of schooling that both produce norms and perpetuate normative practices as grids of intelligibility.

The notion of power is central in attempting to decipher the ways in which the notion of difference is constructed, positioned and dealt with in mainstream settings. The multiplicity and complexity of inclusion cannot be disentangled unless we constantly attempt to tackle the complexity of issues at hand and attempt to formulate hypotheses and give tentative answers to questions such as:

– What are the political dimensions of the 'dilemma of difference'?
– Whose interests are being served when dealing with the 'dilemma of difference'?
– Who decides and on what basis about its resolution?

Theoretical binaries and absolute arbitrations create intellectual, methodological and disciplinary ghettos that imperil 'bridge-building research and scholarship' (Dyson and Howes, 2009: 159), capable of dealing with the highly unpredictable, contingent, value-laden issues pertaining to inclusion. In this respect, the context within which issues around inclusion are at stake acquires a pre-eminent position in any critical endeavour for transformative change. While acknowledging that the existence of certain achievable 'ends' is a theoretical chimera, inclusion should be regarded as being a process and not an 'end', for it necessitates a perennial and reflexive engagement with the host of dynamics impacting upon the policymaking process (Barton, 2008a).

The Education For All caveat, should also be theorized and understood from a different, yet interrelated perspective, that draws a discernible line between developments in inclusive education in countries of the North and the South (developed and developing countries), a topic that will be revisited in chapter 7 in order to discuss *the ways in which* the politics of inclusive education policymaking are played out in developing countries, under the siege of neo-colonialism (Bray, 1993; Nguyen et al., 2009). The Education For All (EFA) movement was instigated by two major world conferences organized by UNESCO, namely Jomtien (1990) and Dakar (2000), and is concerned with increasing educational participation, especially in developing countries where a large proportion of students is denied access to education. Having failed to meet previous targets a decade earlier, many countries were called upon to concentrate on particular areas where progress could be made, and placed a pronounced emphasis on the disproportionate number of girls denied access to education. Disabled people and their advocates were critical over the ways in which they were sidestepped in terms of the priority order of participation in the EFA declarations (UNESCO, 2000; Ainscow and Cesar, 2006). As Miles and Singal (2009: 5) put it in relation to EFA initiatives: 'It is often claimed that disabled children are among the poorest and the most disadvantaged in their communities, and that they have been systematically excluded from more "mainstream" EFA efforts'.

At the same time, however, separate EFA initiatives solely focused on disabled children's rights to education might reinforce erroneous assumptions with regard to the need to devise 'specialist' educational measures and interventions in order to respond to disabled children's right to education. These kind of approaches occasionally reduce children's educational entitlements to segregated and inferior educational arrangements, which provide questionable and impoverished educational opportunities for this group of students. Inclusive education, in this respect, is subsumed within wider initiatives to widen access to questionable forms of education, including special schools. Miles and Singal (2009: 9) cite the example of India whereby EFA initiatives to enhance access to education have been skewed by the proliferation of segregated forms of provision for disabled students, which provide sub-quality education and give rise to 'exclusionary practices and reduced life opportunities' for disabled individuals. Similar trends are manifested in 17 EFA plans from the South and South East Asia region whereby the notion of inclusion is glaringly absent while nonformal, sub-quality education and parochial institutional practices are portrayed as a panacea to meet the educational needs of disadvantaged groups.

EFA initiatives should draw upon the notion of inter-sectionality in order to devise plans responsive to the ways in which disability intersects with other sources of disadvantage (Makkonen, 2002; Miles and Singal, 2009). Disability should be neither tackled as a distinct issue nor subsumed and diluted within the wider remit of EFA initiatives. Initiatives focused exclusively on the notion of disability run the risk of accentuating stigma and discriminatory practices with regard to disabled children, and lose sight of the imperative need to proceed to radical institutional and organizational reform commensurate with the tenets of an inclusive education agenda as part of the EFA initiatives.

Reflective Exercise

Why is inclusion a complex and contested term?

What does it mean to have an inclusive education system?

In what ways does the notion of disability intersect with issues of colour, ethnicity and socioeconomic status?

Outline two perspectives on inclusion and discuss their implications for educational practice.

Summary

The chapter has been concerned with providing an overview of the different theoretical and policy interpretations of inclusion in order to highlight the host of socio-political, historical and ideological dynamics that impact the processes and outcomes of inclusive education policymaking. Inclusion can be understood and theorized in varied ways, something that has significant implications for policy constitution and dissemination. The contradictory and contested policy terrain can be attributed to the multiplicity of meanings ascribed to 'inclusion' and the diverse ways in which it is understood and acted upon by different social actors. As Barton and Armstrong (2007: 6) write: 'The concepts and ideas involved in debates concerning inclusive education are subject to struggles over their meaning and application', and this has a prodigious effect on the ways in which inclusive education policy is created, defined and implemented.

Useful Websites

Centre for Studies on Inclusive Education
    www.csie.org.uk/
Index for Inclusion: Developing Learning and Participation in Schools
    www.eenet.org.uk/resources/docs/Index%20English.pdf
Alliance for Inclusive Education
    www.allfie.org.uk
Enabling Education Network (EENET)
    www.eenet.org.uk/
Excluded/ Vulnerable Groups/ Right to Education Project
    www.right-to-education.org/node/47
EFA Global Monitoring Report? Education/United Nations – UNESCO
    www.unesco.org/new/en/education/themes/leading-the-international-agenda/efareport/

2

Pedagogy for Inclusion

Introduction

The question as to whether there is pedagogy for inclusion and what it entails will be discussed and analysed in this chapter. The notion of pedagogy constitutes an important dimension of inclusive schools. Teachers' pedagogy is at the heart of teaching and learning and, hence, at the heart of an inclusive education framework concerned with respecting and providing for learners' diverse needs and abilities.

The concept of inclusion presupposes schools that are socially just in terms of learning and participation. The 'politics of identity' underpinning the struggles towards greater inclusive policies and practices can be achieved by adopting socially just pedagogies (Goodley, 2007) intended to provide equal opportunities for learning and participation in non-discriminatory learning environments. Socially just pedagogies entail diversifying and changing the curriculum, teaching methods, structures, cultures and practices of current schooling, in order to meet learner diversity.

Inclusive pedagogy: a paradigm shift

As discussed in the previous chapter, the notion of inclusive education predicated on a human rights approach to disability and difference constitutes an ideological shift that moves beyond categorization and labelling, and seeks to address the socio-political dimensions of special educational needs and disabilities. An inclusive and, hence, a democratic school should represent 'new social settlements that liberate us from the yoke of fortresses buttressed by traditional special education thinking and practice' (Slee, 2001a: 385–6). That said, the failure of some groups of students is not solely attributed to individual deficits, but also to the existing inflexible and monodimensional school structures and cultures that unwittingly exclude and marginalize certain groups of students (OFSTED, 2005).

Central to this new ideology is the notion of equality of opportunity and the creation of comprehensive education systems that presuppose the participation of all students in learning and cultural communities of mainstream schools (Booth and Ainscow, 2002), where the value and well-being of all students are prioritized. Towards this end, educational settings need to be underpinned by a radically new ideology of thinking and acting where diversity is the norm (Skrtic, 1994; Karagiannis et al., 1998) and considered as part of human experience (Ballard, 1995; Ainscow, 1998).

Inclusive schools are concerned with embracing and responding to learner diversity in effective ways, while disabled students are no longer subjected to the normalizing effects of a deficit-oriented gaze endemic to assimilationist learning environments (Booth and Ainscow, 1998). Difference is valued and 'celebrated' (Barton, 1997), while practices that place disabled people in a 'less than a human' position are denounced. The new pedagogical ethos, as Chrinstensen (1996: 77) suggests, recognizes all students as 'reflecting a diversity of cultural, social, racial, physical and intellectual identities'.

Based on empirical evidence documenting the failure of special schools to provide for students' needs, notwithstanding the generous funding allocated to them, Thomas (1997: 103) asserts 'that inclusive schools are good for all children'. More recently, a systematic review of international research pointed to the fact that inclusive settings benefitted students across a range of special educational needs (Canadian Council on Learning, 2009; cited in Long et al., 2011).

Within an inclusive education setting, diversity in classrooms can potentially enrich and enhance the learning experience and offer diverse and novel opportunities for learning not only for disabled children but for all children where their 'capabilities and unique needs' are met in 'humane and effective ways' (Stainback and Stainback, 1996: xi). This can only be achieved when schools manage to become more responsive to diversity by identifying specific organizational and learning support structures necessary to promote equality in opportunity and outcome (Starkey, 1991: 205) commensurate with students' wide spectrum of capabilities and needs.

Inclusive education is concerned with providing quality mainstream education for all students and, hence, any links with special education should be jettisoned. As Corbett (2001: 13) suggests, inclusive education is not a 'merger of special and regular education'. Despite acknowledging some beneficial aspects of specialist instruction to promoting inclusion, these approaches should be merely seen as being part of providing a diverse repertoire of teaching approaches and learning strategies in order to enhance the learning and participation of all pupils in inclusive mainstream classrooms.

It is occasionally the case that successful pedagogical practices traditionally used in special education are uncritically rejected. It is suggested that some of these practices can be a valuable means of supporting inclusion (Corbett and Norwich, 1999) without, however, finding recourse to 'quick fixes' linked to deficit-oriented and compensatory measures of support. An indicative example of these pedagogical practices is the instructional strategy TEACCH (Treatment and Education of Autistic and other Communication handicapped Children) devised by a nationwide learning and support project conducted at the University of North Carolina in the 1970s, in order to help students with autism overcome organizational barriers and access the curriculum (Mesibov and Howley, 2003).

Inclusive education should be seen as the new impetus for schools in order to improve and become more effective in terms of teaching and learning (Ekins and Grimes, 2009: 88). However, in order to achieve this, schools need a radical reform whereby they should reconsider their curricula designs, structure, teaching approaches, organization strategies and collaborative practices with a view to becoming more responsive to learner diversity. The concept of educational differentiation holds the key in order to accommodate learner diversity in informed and effective ways.

As far as learner diversity in terms of ability is concerned, considerable research evidence highlights the fact that there is no separate/distinct pedagogy for teaching students with special educational needs and/or disabilities. Nevertheless, some specific/ specialist pedagogical approaches can potentially improve the learning outcomes of some students (Norwich and Lewis,

2001; Davies and Florian, 2004; Norwich, 2008b). These specialist teaching approaches can constitute part of educational differentiation, without, however, the latter being limited to these approaches. Thus the concept of differentiation entails a multidimensional approach to providing continuing and varied support for learning by means of graduated and carefully monitored educational differentiation.

The first stage of differentiation should be informed by the principles of the Universal Design for Learning (UDL) (Rose, 2001; Rose and Mayer, 2002; Burgstahler and Cory, 2008), followed by more direct/focused and individualized modes of differentiation, whereby the notion of personalized learning should underpin and inform all stages. The latter has been defined as follows:

> [Personalized learning] is not individualised learning where pupils sit alone. Nor is it pupils left to their own devices – which too often reinforces low aspirations. It means shaping teaching around the way different youngsters learn; it means taking care to nurture the unique talents of every pupil. (DfES, 2004b: 2)

The aim of the following section is to examine the current understandings regarding inclusive pedagogy both at a macro and micro level, in terms of whole-school policy and in terms of teaching and learning within classrooms. Pedagogy, in strict terms, focuses on the teacher's role and activity. Certain views on pedagogy, however, propose a different and a rather complex model that consists of a plethora of interactive elements that go beyond the classroom and the teacher, namely institutional resources, school ethos/vision and communities values. Within this framework, pedagogy is to be understood as the result of the nature of the relations and interactions between the various elements of the model (Watkins and Mortimore, 1999; Corbett, 2001). Consequently, it can be argued that pedagogy is closely linked with the wider school organization, structure and ethos and, hence, it should be seen not only as a part of a whole school policy but also as a direct result of it.

Educational differentiation for socially just and non-discriminatory learning

The purpose of this section is to present and explain the theoretical, policy and practical aspects of differentiation in order to devise and implement socially just and non-discriminatory pedagogies in inclusive classrooms. The aim is to provide a rationale for adopting the model of multilevel and graduated differentiation intended to meet the needs of all students without finding recourse in segregation and discriminatory educational practices. The model of graduated differentiation can act as a safety valve in order to avoid differentiation strategies which might 'impoverish' the curriculum and stigmatize certain individuals on the basis of their presumed inability to follow conventional educational programmes.

Inclusive education entails creating schools that are socially just in terms of learning and participation. Socially just schools have as their main point of departure the notion of differentiated instruction that requires the modification of the curriculum, teaching structures, cultures and practices of mainstream schools, according to the needs, abilities, experiences, biographies and diverse developmental trajectories of students. The notion of differentiation also entails touching upon and developing students' unique characteristics and capabilities in order to maximize learning. Westwood (2001) warns us against adopting differentiation strategies that can impoverish the curriculum by providing less challenging material and coursework.

The Individuals with Disability Act in the United States of America stipulates that students with disabilities must have instructional opportunities that ensure their access and progress in general curriculum (Rothstein and Johnson, 2010). This legislative caveat is crucially important because 'any approach that suggests giving "less" to some students is open to criticism under principles of equity and social justice' (Westwood, 2001: 6). By no means should the aim be to remove learning challenges and provide inferior educational experiences through compensatory measures of support. Rather, the aim should be to remove the barriers to participation and provide access to learning (Lloyd, 2008) through more inclusive pedagogical designs.

The issue of whether to categorize students with disabilities and/or SEN or not has been another important and widely debated issue that focuses on whether the categorization of children according to their educational needs is a useful and necessary strategy in order to respond to students' needs in effective ways (Wilson, 2000; Hollenweger, 2008; Norwich, 2008b). The process of categorization not only entails the danger of stigmatizing and labelling certain individuals, but also entails the danger of engendering low expectations and adopting a very restricted repertoire of teaching strategies for certain groups of students, premised on the erroneous assumption that these strategies are effective for particular groups of students. Notwithstanding that some specific pedagogical strategies might be effective for some categories of students (e.g., students with dyslexia, autism), these strategies do not constitute an educational panacea for all students who belong to a particular category of disability and special educational needs (Norwich, 2008b). The process of categorization imposes a particular kind of mindset – a negative mindset most of the times – about certain groups of pupils while in essence the various groups are 'cross-cutting, fluid and shifting' (Young, 1990: 45).

Consequently, students' educational needs are not delimited to the broad characteristics and needs ascribed to certain categories of disability or difficulty. This position is indicative of the broad and overlapping nature of disability categories as they are currently utilized (Holleneger, 2008; Norwich, 2008b), something that challenges the alleged pedagogical effectiveness of categorization on the basis of disability (Burke and Ruedel, 2008). Some countries according to Holleneger (2008) have already changed their service provision with a view to devising and offering cross-categorical programmes, one example being the Common Assessment Framework (CAF) (DfES, 2006) introduced in the United Kingdom, which is underpinned by a non-categorical approach, whereby special educational needs are understood within their wider context of reciprocally related factors and dynamics (development of the child, parenting, family and environmental factors). Lewis and Norwich (2001) suggest that the best way of categorizing students for educational purposes can be determined by the learning styles of students.

Additionally, in attempting to provide some guidelines as to the optimal ways in which the dilemma of difference can be dealt with, Norwich (2002, 2010) suggests that in the first stage we should take into consideration students' common needs and characteristics. In the same way, O' Brien (1998) points to the fact that there are educational needs that are common regardless of the physical, emotional, social and cognitive difficulties that some students might encounter. Therefore, as emphasized by Norwich and Corbett (1998: 85), differentiation should be perceived as being a multidimensional concept because it has to do with the 'multi-dimensional concept of educational needs as the basis for connecting special and mainstream education' on the basis of several dimensions of need. It is suggested that:

> The separatist perspective should be replaced by one which sees all pupils including those with SEN in terms of several dimensions of need: 1. as having educational needs which they share with all pupils; 2. as having needs which arise from their exceptional characteristics, such as impairments or particular abilities; and 3. as having needs which are unique to them as individuals and which distinguish

them from all others including those with the same impairments or abilities. (Norwich and Corbett, 1998: 87–8)

In alignment with the above considerations, the revised 2001 SEN Code of Practice (DfES, 2001) for England and Wales refers to the need to adopt a graduated response to special educational needs, whereby the notion of differentiation should not be regarded as being a special educational intervention, but it should constitute an indispensable component of quality first teaching. Similarly, the 'waves of intervention model' promotes the idea of progressive and systematic intervention at a number of levels (DfE, 2011). The first 'wave' of intervention refers to quality first teaching through differentiation, the second to a more focused and targeted differentiation intended for some groups of pupils in order to catch up with their peers, while the third 'wave' refers to individualized differentiation and intervention that can be achieved with the involvement of various SEN professionals within the framework of multi-agency cooperation in order to enhance learning (DfES, 2001; 2003b).

In a similar way, the Individuals with Disabilities Act (IDEA, 2004) in the United States of America promotes a multi-tiered Response to Intervention (RTI) or, as otherwise referred to, Response to Instruction, the aim being to reduce special educational referrals for students whose learning difficulties can be attributed to 'poor' or 'inadequate' instruction. RTI is an approach that moves away from the notion of categories and special interventions and concentrates on providing an appropriate, high quality and effective education for all students, including students with disabilities.

The first 'tier' of response is concerned with providing high quality and evidence-based instruction for all children in general classrooms. The early intervention caveat is also applied at this stage through universal screening assessments in order to single out students at risk in terms of reading and behaviour. 'Tier two' refers to targeted small group instructions and additional assistance provided by teachers in general classrooms, intended for those students who might have problems in specific skill areas. These targeted interventions should be brief (around six weeks) and children's progress should be constantly monitored. Finally, 'Tier three' focuses on very intensive instruction intended for students who do not make adequate progress in Tier two. This final stage might also entail assessment in order to determine eligibility for special education provision (Rothstein and Johnson, 2010; McLaughlin, 2009).

Given the above considerations, the notion of differentiation presupposes that teachers must first develop learning programmes and activities based on quality first teaching and evidence-based pedagogical principles (US, Senate, 2001; Mitchell, 2008) in order to provide accessible and effective learning environments in ordinary classrooms, with a view to minimizing the need for specific interventions and compensatory measures of support. However, as the various differentiated stages of intervention suggest, more targeted changes in curricula and activities, with the use of more focused and specialist differentiated instruction, might be still necessary for some students (Ellis et al., 2008). As stated by Mace (1998), who was actually the proponent of the Universal Design for Learning (UDL) intended to enhance educational accessibility for all students without the need for specialist interventions and adaptations:

> nothing can be truly universal; there will always be people who cannot use an item no matter how thoughtfully it is designed. However, we can always improve on the things we design to make them more universally usable. (cited in Mc Guire et al., 2006: 172)

The above extract connotes the importance of paying attention to individualized differentiation, which should inform and underpin all levels of differentiated instruction. As Rose and Meyer (2000: 4) write:

> To many people the term seems to imply that UDL is a quest for a single, one-size-fits-all solution that will work for everyone. In fact, the very opposite is true. The essence of UDL is flexibility and the inclusion of alternatives to adapt to the myriad variations in learner needs, styles and preferences.

In relation to the latter point, the UDL enables teachers to adopt the cyclical process of design, analysis and reflection. This process entails adopting continuous evaluation of the content and process of teaching in order to provide specialized and personalized support to students when and where needed (Thousand et al., 2006). The use and combination of different kinds and levels of differentiation is essential so as to address issues of accessibility and support in effective and efficient ways, something that can be achieved through the model of graduated differentiation.

The first part of this section below will deal with the theoretical principles of UDL, along with its implications for educational practice. The second part will be given over to exploring more intensive, focused and personalized forms of differentiation.

> ### Reflective Exercises
>
> Can you identify the dangers lurking behind the recognition of 'difference'?
>
> In what ways can mainstream schools respond to learner diversity in non-discriminatory ways?

The principles of Universal Design for Learning (UDL)

The principles of Universal Design for Learning (UDL) have emerged from the field of architecture and developed by the Center for Applied Special Technology (CAST) in the United States of America. The introduction of anti-discrimination legislation with regard to disability, has highlighted the social barriers disabled individuals encounter in their daily lives (Burgstahler and Cory, 2008). The application of UDL in education has been concerned with the introduction of teaching methods so as to enhance educational accessibility for all students without the need for specialist interventions and adaptations. To this end, the whole process entails strategically designing courses and devising teaching methods intended to meet learner diversity on the basis of ability, learning style, race, ethnicity and other characteristics, without finding recourse in special educational practices. The process involves several practical ways of teaching using a variety of methods, including the use of technology, in order to present new information while incorporating approaches and theoretical perspectives akin to the principles of inclusive education, such as the need to promote collaborative learning and multi-sensory teaching, taking into consideration insights from the theory of multiple intelligences and learning styles. The Universal Design for Learning provides teachers a solid knowledge and a conceptual and practical platform to utilize and build upon learner diversity in order to improve teaching and learning (Thousand et al., 2006).

Rose (2001) sets out the three axes underpinning the overall design, which presuppose a good theoretical and empirical understanding of the varied ways in which students differ. An important dimension of learner diversity, as explained by Meyer and Rose (2000), is related to the ways in which learners recognize information. The authors provide the example of Einstein, whose cortex of recognition system was disproportionately distributed in spatial cognition. This explains why Einstein had difficulty in recognizing the relationship between letters and sounds while he was a prodigy in understanding and exemplifying the most difficult theories of physics. Each key area is proposed as a means to minimizing learning barriers and maximizing learning through a flexible and multidimensional response to the needs, capabilities, intelligences and learning styles of students. Specifically, these principles are intended: (1) To promote multiple and flexible methods of presentation by teaching through multiple intelligences (Gardner, 1983), Logical/Mathematical, Verbal/Linguistic, Bodily/Kinesthetic, Visual/Spatial, Interpersonal, Intrapersonal, Naturalist, Existentialist; (2) To promote flexible methods of participation and learning outcomes; and (3) to promote diverse and flexible methods and possibilities of expression in order to enhance students' metacognitive capabilities and cultivate and develop diverse types of intelligences.

Effective teaching requires flexibility in the presentation of concepts using multiple methods and materials responsive to students' learning styles. With reference to differentiating teaching based on the theory of multiple intelligences (MI), Armstrong (2009: 57) gives the following simple example:

> Even traditional linguistic teaching can take place in a variety of ways designed to stimulate the eight intelligences. The teacher who lectures with rhythmic emphasis (musical), draws pictures on the board to illustrate points (spatial), makes dramatic gestures as she talks (bodily-kinaesthetic), pauses to give pupils time to reflect (intrapersonal), asks questions that invite spirited interaction (interpersonal) and includes references to nature in her lectures (naturalist) is using MI principles within a traditional teacher-centred perspective

Effective teaching also entails multiple options for participation in the learning process. The various modes of interaction of students with the teaching material can either facilitate or inhibit learning. It is important that students are afforded ample and diverse opportunities in order to select their preferred modalities of learning new material, which in turn should be adapted in order to meet their diverse interests, biographies and experiences. Also, the teaching material should have varied levels of challenge so as to be responsive to a wide range of capabilities and needs (Burgstahler and Cory, 2008). For example, for gifted and talented students enrichment and extension activities should be added to the existing programme of study so as to diversify and maximize learning (Senior and Whybra, 2005). Students should also be given ample opportunities to have access to multiple ways of expression in documenting what they have learnt. For instance, students in Key stages 1 and 2, who have difficulty in writing, can articulate their thoughts and knowledge orally, while some others can write a play, act out a role play, or complete a project in order to demonstrate their learning. Moreover, new technology can be utilized in order to remove disabling barriers, namely speech-to-text software or the deployment of virtual spaces in order to enable students to communicate in a variety of modalities (via typing, symbol choice, or voice recognition) (Long et al., 2011).

As we have seen earlier, teachers first need to develop ways to diversify their teaching based on the principles of UDL in order to minimize the need for specialist interventions. Norwich (2008b) does not propose any specific educational interventions for children with SEN and points to the fact that the common and individual needs of students are more important for devising and selecting educational interventions. What he simply proposes is a continuum of pedagogical approaches thereby indicating the need for clearer, directed and more intensive ways of teaching children with learning difficulties, without, however, these ways being qualitatively different from those used for all children. As Norwich (2008b: 137) argues, the intensification of teaching along the continuum involves more 'intensive strategies, for example, more practice or more examples of concepts'.

Woodward et al. (2001) draw on research evidence in order to suggest that the adoption of intensive teaching methods in Numeracy was crucial for the success of students with learning difficulties. In a similar manner, Mitchell (2008) lists direct instruction among the most effective teaching strategies in order to enhance learning for all students. Direct and explicit teaching entails frequent opportunities to practice targeted activities, ongoing assessment for learning and gradual withdrawal of learning support (Davies and Miyake, 2004).

However, it needs noting that the intensification of teaching methods along the continuum of pedagogical approaches might indicate that the different methods of instruction are no longer a matter of 'degree' or 'intensity', but perhaps of kind, something that requires more specialist knowledge in terms of differentiation (Norwich and Lewis, 2007; Norwich, 2008a). Thus the modification of instruction and activities using specialist differentiated instruction may be necessary for some students.

To this end, Norwich (2008b), based on evidence from a longitudinal study, points to the fact that the needs of certain groups of students can be best met through the adoption of specific teaching approaches. Some categories of disability may require more specialist knowledge and, therefore, more specialist teaching methods. In a similar vein, Davies and Florian (2004: 6) conducted a study commissioned by the then Department for Education and Skills in the UK (Research Report RR516) and concluded that:

> The teaching approaches and strategies identified during the review were not sufficiently differentiated from those used for teaching all children to justify a distinctive SEN pedagogy. This does not diminish the importance of special education knowledge, but highlights it as an essential component of pedagogy.

Arguably, there are some teaching methods that may be particularly effective for some groups of students and, hence, educators might need to have some sort of specialist pedagogical awareness so as to have adequate knowledge base for designing and using appropriate teaching approaches (Mitchell, 2008). This of course, does not mean that educational decisions about teaching strategies are uncritically driven by specialist knowledge and specific approaches that may be effective for particular groups of students. The pedagogical approaches must be devised in order to be responsive to the common needs of children and adapted to their individual needs, a process that should be at the heart of decisions on educational differentiation (Norwich and Lewis, 2007).

Mitchell (2008: 7) exemplifies some differentiation strategies for specific groups of students, such as students with autism who need some kind of differentiated instruction in order to meet their specific needs. Autistic spectrum disorders are associated with a range of difficulties and differences typically related to the core skills in reciprocal social interaction, social communication and imagination, and repetitive behaviour (Wing, 1996). As already discussed, traditional special education programmes like TEACCH, are very beneficial for these students (Mitchell, 2008). The same applies to Applied Behavioural Analysis (ABA) that has played an instrumental role in developing precision teaching approaches for students with autism (Long et al., 2011). Adopting these principles in conjunction with other simple educational strategies of differentiated teaching like social stories and Circle Time can bring to bear very positive outcomes for this group of students, as well as for other students in inclusive classrooms (Lewis and Norwich, 2005; Rose and Howley, 2007).

As far as the individualized needs of students are concerned, these should be registered on their Individual Educational Plans or, as alternatively called, Individualized Educational Plans (IEPs), which delineate the services needed by pupils designated as having SEN, so as to focus on some very specific learning difficulties they might encounter and which go beyond any common characteristics or difficulties faced by other students. This stage is implemented after exhausting all kinds of differentiated teaching. For example, the difficulties faced by a student with speech and language problems can be minimized by using very specific forms of symbolic communication carefully selected to meet her individual needs, such as the Pictures Exchange Communication System (PECS), or the sign and symbols language Makaton, Pictograms and Ideograms for Communication (PIC-Pictogram Ideogram Communication) (Mitchell, 2008).

> ### Reflective Exercise
>
> Why does inclusive education necessitate a critical re-consideration of the notion of pedagogy?
>
> Why is a graduated response to disability and special educational needs important?
>
> Are there common educational practices that can be adopted for all students irrespective of their diverse needs?

Inclusive pedagogy and teachers' professionalism

A key feature of inclusive education is the eradication of exclusion (Booth, 1995), something that requires fundamental changes in thinking regarding differences that are not merely to be tolerated but also to be positively valued and celebrated. This entails developing and instilling a culture that respects and valorises difference as an enriching aspect of teaching and learning. This aspect of institutional reform is exemplified in the first stage of the Index for Inclusion (Booth and Ainscow, 2002). The Index offers a comprehensive guidance to schools in order to initiate and implement a process of inclusive school development.

The Index encourages schools to adopt self-assessment to analyse and develop their inclusive cultures, policies and practices. In terms of developing inclusive cultures, schools are expected to devise and enforce a plan concerned with the ways in which students should feel welcomed and supported, thereby fostering 'a school culture which recognizes and values differences' (Corbett, 2001: 23) within which everybody has the same educational rights and opportunities to reach his/her full potential in effective and welcoming learning communities. An important constituent element of the latter is the positive relationship and educative alchemy between the learner and the teacher (Cornwall, 1997). As the *Cambridge Review* (Alexander, 2009: 4) on the condition and future of primary education in the United Kingdom has suggested:

> We want to strengthen what, according to international research, separates the best teachers from the rest: their depth of knowledge of and engagement with what is to be taught, the quality and cognitive power of the classroom interaction they orchestrate, and their skill in assessing and providing feedback on pupils' learning – all day, every day.

However, 'the quality and cognitive power of the classroom interaction' is occasionally undermined by negative views that many teachers hold about inclusion (Avramidis and Norwich, 2002) as they occasionally find intimidating the possibility of having children with diverse needs in their classroom (Jordan and Powell, 1995; Florian et al., 1998). This is not surprising given that teachers are also 'pathologized' by the neo-liberal discourse (Beck, 1999; Karlsen, 2000; Sleeter, 2008) as they are increasingly rendered accountable to meet certain 'standards' gauged against 'perfomativity' indicators (Ball, 2009). This is a powerful circle of subordination that exacerbates the ethical dilemmas (Cranston et al., 2005) of those who are at the forefront of the struggles for inclusion, for they are expected to compromise contradictory policy agendas and align concerns for equity and social justice with neo-liberal constructions of educational excellence (Taylor, 2004). Sleeter (2008: 1947) analyses the 'neoliberal assaults on Teacher Education' which:

> aim not only to deprofessionalize teaching by devaluing professional preparation of teachers, but also to undermine equity and democracy by restructuring education around corporate needs . . . The move toward testing shifts power to determine what it means to learn and teach away from educators, and toward legislatures and corporations that produce and sell tests.

Ball (2009: 51) cites some quotations from *The Guardian* (9 January 2001) in order to document the struggles and dilemmas experienced by teachers in the pursuit of preordained 'performance indicators', who as 'ethical subjects find their values challenged or displaced by the "terrors of performativity"'.

> What happened to my creativity? What happened to my professional integrity? What happened to the fun in teaching and learning? What happened?
>
> I was a primary school teacher for 22 years but I left in 1996 because I was not prepared to sacrifice the children for the glory of politicians and their business plans for education. (Ball, 2009: 51)

Teachers should be empowered to enhance their professional expertise and autonomy if they are to create, through the transformative potentials of their pedagogies, a paradigm shift from the vestiges of special education that undermine the transformative potentials of pedagogy. This can be significantly achieved through what Howes et al. (2009: 31) call a 'professional development for inclusion' that

> involves teachers in challenging the constraints around their practice, even while they themselves are subject to those constraints. Teachers taking action and challenging the expectations and assumptions which constitute the status quo . . . Professional development for inclusion involves a discussion of values. We are drawn to a principled definition of inclusion, and a view that inclusion necessarily involves working out those principles in action. (Howes et al., 2009: 31–2)

This aspect of teachers' professional development embodies the critical dimension of transformative change and necessitates interrogating attitudes and ideological underpinnings with regard to disability and difference, along with the ways in which they affect teachers' language, writing and acting in relation to certain groups of students (Pihlaja, 2007). As Ballard (2004) contends, inclusion is primarily about ourselves and the ways in which we understand, conceptualize, interpret and enact inclusion. Similarly, Allan (2003: 171) reminds us of the necessity to interrogate the ways in which our 'actions create barriers to inclusion' and she urges us not to conjure up inclusive education as a project referring 'to a discrete population of children, but rather (as) something we must do to ourselves' (Allan 2005: 293). In this respect Graham and Slee (2008a: 280) point to the necessity to adopt critical perspectives and ask ourselves uncomfortable questions with respect to disability and difference.

For instance, critical pedagogy (Freire, 1970; Giroux, 1992; MacLaren, 1998) proclaims the emancipatory and anti-oppressive possibilities of schooling and pedagogy, whereby the notion of pedagogy is theorized as a means to proceed to transformative change. Educational professionals can be characterized as the embodiments of critical pedagogy and as Giroux (2003: 10). points out, 'Educators should reject forms of schooling that marginalize pupils who are poor, black and least advantaged'. Even though critical pedagogy has significantly omitted to refer to the issue of disability on par with class, gender and race, it nonetheless provides useful insights into the critical dimension of pedagogy and its potential to abolish oppressive structures and ideologies within schooling. It needs noting, however, that the notion of critical pedagogy has been criticized on the grounds that it does not take into consideration the subtleties of the classrooms and the multifarious dynamics that impinge upon pedagogy and social justice (Gabel, 2002). Effective pedagogies entail the ability to discern the dynamic and ever-changing realities of classroom contexts and respond to them in informed ways. These pedagogies go beyond catastrophic binaries of 'normality' and 'abnormality' that alienate and ostracize certain groups of students. This necessitates interrogating personal values and ethics, along with the ways in which they are conveyed and reified through pedagogical practices The latter can be either 'emancipatory' or 'subjugating', 'potentiating' or disabling (e.g., Claxton and Carr, 2004; Goodley, 2007).

The critical dimension of pedagogy requires a robust knowledge base around the complex and contested nature of inclusion (Lingard and Mills, 2007) and also ample space for educational practitioners, policymakers and other stakeholders to pursue personal and professional development in order to reflect upon their educational practice (Schön, 1983; Pollard, 2008; Scales et al., 2011). In so doing, they will be enabled to resolve a host of dilemmas in relation to their role in fostering inclusive pedagogies. This is particularly true for teachers 'who control access to the curriculum; whose assumptions, hopes or fears about young people help to create or dispose chances for them' (Howes et al., 2009: 15).

It is therefore very important that teachers are empowered to interrogate and ultimately challenge their own 'pathologizing' values and beliefs, which engender and consolidate disabling pedagogies, so as to bring out the potential of those students who would have otherwise failed given the neo-liberal trends and blame-the-victim imperatives endemic to contemporary schooling. As Ball (2007: 191) suggests:

> We need to struggle to think differently about education policy before it is too late. We need to move beyond the tyrannies of improvement, efficiency and

standards, to recover a language of and for education articulated in terms of ethics, moral obligations and values.

The quest for inclusion, as an ethical project necessitates 'exercising the desire for something other than the status quo' (Allan, 2005: 293), a venture that involves subverting inequalities of power by providing a critical analysis of the ways in which the notion of 'difference', and the negative connotations associated to it, have been construed, become consolidated and perpetuated. This kind of critical engagement can potentially interrogate and deconstruct the multitude of disabling pedagogies that fail a significant number of students who are regarded 'as eternally lacking (desiring subjects consuming the things they lack)' (Goodley, 2007: 321).

Even though this kind of critical engagement should not be regarded as a panacea, it is, nevertheless, significant to the attempts to foster inclusive pedagogies. As Nayler and Keddie (2007: 201) write: 'This is not to say that enhanced and sophisticated teacher reflection alone will overturn social injustice. What we do claim, however, is that enhanced teacher interrogation of practice will support teachers to make strategic decisions in relation to their pedagogies'. Allan (2004: 428) draws on Foucault's and Derrida's ethics in order to highlight the necessity to be vigilant and 'fight against accumulation, concentration and monopoly; in short, against all quantitative phenomena that might marginalize or reduce to silence anything that cannot be measured on their scale'.

Taking as an example the United Kingdom context, there is much scepticism over the ways in which teachers' professionalism is currently portrayed and gauged against prescribed 'professional standards' and career development thresholds (Furlong, 2008; Beck, 2009). Beck (2009) discusses the trainability and technicist regimes underpinning the current specification of professional standards (TDA, 2007). Not surprisingly,

> The cumulative effect of this form of discourse is profoundly reductive: it suggests that being a professional educator is a matter of acquiring a limited corpus of state prescribed knowledge accompanied by a set of similarly prescribed skills and competencies. (Beck, 2009: 8)

Similarly in the United States of America, Sleeter (2008: 1953) discusses the impact of government-mandated testing on teacher education programmes:

> In this context, teacher education programmes are being compelled to jettison not only explicit equity-oriented teacher preparation, but also learner-centered teaching, in order to prepare technicians who can implement curriculum packages.

Teachers' professionalism should not be delimited to conventional notions of technical rationality and competence-based training regimes that fail to take into consideration the ethical dimension of teaching and pedagogy. The notions of ethics and ethical knowledge – what Foucault (2000: 108) calls an 'antifascistic ethics' – necessitate, according to McWhorter (2005: xvi), 'recognizing and challenging the fascism in us all, in our heads and in our everyday behaviour' – with a view to subverting a host of oppressive pedagogies endemic to current schooling. In this respect, Allan (2004) reconceptualizes teachers' professional identities within the context of inclusion whereby teachers:

> . . . will have to contend with the ethics of their encounter with the other. The key question facing student teachers is how they engage with the marginalised or silenced other without trying to assimilate or acculturate that other. (Allan, 2004: 428)

The quest for inclusion necessitates a serious engagement with the ways in which the role of teachers and their pedagogies can be reconfigured and appropriated in alignment with the demands of an inclusive educational agenda. Mounting research evidence suggests that good teachers have a massive impact on students' learning. As it is stated in the Schools White Paper 2010 on The Importance of Teaching in the United Kingdom:

> Studies in the United States have shown that an individual pupil taught for three consecutive years by a teacher in the top ten per cent of performance can make as much as two years more progress than a pupil taught for the same period by a teacher in the bottom ten per cent of performance. (DfES, 2010: 19)

Hence, drawing on the McKinsey Report (2007: 29) on improving school systems across the globe, the great challenge is to instil in 'thousands of teachers the capacity and knowledge to deliver that great instruction reliably, every day across thousands of schools, in circumstances that vary enormously from one classroom to the next – and all of this with very little oversight (Furlong, 2008: 732). Obviously, this is a great challenge that needs to be pursued in greater magnitude and depth than the current teachers' professional standards project and prescribe.

Reflective Exercise

What is (should be) the role of teachers in current schooling, and how are they empowered to promote inclusive education?

Summary

Based on the need to provide quality education for all children without discriminatory and segregating practices, the concept of differentiation must constitute an integral component of quality teaching. This entails the ability of teachers to be acquainted with and draw upon a variety of pedagogical approaches to adequately meet the needs of all students. The adoption of very specific pedagogical approaches and intervention strategies requires some additional knowledge and expertise, and presupposes seamless cooperation between teachers and other professionals in order to design and implement intervention strategies. Of course, these individualized interventions must be brief and effective, so as not to monopolize the educational experiences of students with disabilities. The important thing is to find, according to Ekins and Grimes (2009: 88):

> the right balance between providing the right support for children to enable them to make progress and ensuring that they have their entitled access to a broad and balanced curriculum, where they are able to enjoy and excel in other curriculum areas.

For instance in Finland, additional support provided in part-time special education placements last for a short period of time (4–10 weeks). This kind of support can be provided on a proactive and preventive basis, in the sense that the system does not wait for the student to 'fail' in order to provide additional learning support. Another interesting point is that this support is open to every student who, for various reasons, might encounter problems with learning, without the need for 'administrative decision' or 'diagnosis'. In this way the Finish educational system has build, according to Graham and Jahnukainen (2011: 279), 'a more inclusive system by default'. This has been achieved through an effective 'fully comprehensive school' without adopting the 'rhetoric of inclusion', which can be occasionally reduced to discriminatory practices of categorization and diagnosis.

Useful Websites

Universal Design for Learning
   www.cast.org/udl/
National Center on Universal Design and Learning
   www.udlcenter.org/

3

Special Education
Policymaking: A Critique

Introduction

This chapter aims to question and destabilize unidimensional and deficit-oriented perspectives upon which special education policy has been historically predicated, and provide alternative explanations to individual and medical perspectives. By adopting a pluralistic theoretical framework, the attempt is to question the historical orthodoxies informing special education policy and practice, and offer an alternative theory of special education.

Special education policymaking cannot be adequately theorized unless examined and analyzed against a backdrop of different theoretical conceptualizations and constructs that can illuminate the complex nature of the issues at hand. In particular, postmodern and poststructural accounts (Peters,

1999) are eclectically deployed with a view to offering 'emancipatory alternatives' that can potentially open up new possibilities for special education policy analysis (Skrtic, 1991; Gallagher, 2001; Thomas and Loxley, 2007). The utilization of post-functional accounts can provide an alternative theory of special education that entails challenging individual pathology imperatives and deficit-based assumptions.

An alternative theory of special education brings to the surface the power/knowledge couplet that arguably constitutes to a significant extent what has come to be known as special education. Postmodern and poststructural analyses provide alternative insights into the nature of disability and special educational needs and open up new analytical avenues in order to question and reposition taken-for-granted assumptions and understandings with regard to special education policy and practice (see the following sections for a comprehensive analysis of postmodern and poststructural scholarship). These alternative theorizations of special education draw significantly on the work of French philosopher Michel Foucault (1979; 1980a,b; 1984a; 1999) whose work can be located in both disciplinary camps (postmodern and poststructural).

While acknowledging the relative and contingent nature of knowledge that is inexorably bound up with power relations, these analyses provide significant insights into the political nature of special education policymaking and the host of socio-political and historical dynamics that give rise to notions of 'disability' and 'special educational needs', and generate exclusionary and discriminatory practices.

Farrell (2009) is especially critical towards theoretical frameworks that draw upon these alternative perspectives and fail to acknowledge the effectiveness of some aspects of a special education knowledge base. He cites the work of Loxley and Thomas (2007) as an example of adopting a partisan perspective on theorizing inclusive education, while denouncing empirical evidence supporting the beneficial outcomes of some aspects of special education. Even if we assume that this is an acceptable empirical scenario, providing an alternative theory of special education is still a useful and much needed theoretical perspective intended to act as a disciplinary antidote to the longstanding predominance of psychology and medicine in the field.

Going even further, Kauffman and Sasso (2006: 65) characterize postmodern theorizing as 'intellectually bankrupt' that 'leads to catastrophic consequences for any field of study, including special education'. Sasso (2001) suggests that this kind of theorizing has no value in informing educational practice and might have a detrimental effect on it. As a counterargument to these kind of assertions, Slee (1997: 416) regards theoretical importations intended to provide alternative understandings of disability and special educational needs (SEN) as an 'act of restoration' aimed at unveiling the 'structure of power and social relations and their mediation through the ethos and activity of education'.

The aim of providing an alternative theory of special education is to facilitate what Foucault (1980a: 82) calls 'the insurrection of subjugated knowledges' that have been traditionally excluded from dominant analyses of disability and special educational needs. These 'knowledges' denounce theoretical dogmatism and conceptual monopolies and seek to establish diversity and interrogate the core elements underpinning the incessant struggles over greater inclusive education policy and practice. By no means is the aim here to dogmatically impose the unassailability of particular theoretical and analytical frameworks, but rather, the aim is to highlight the necessity to avoid monolithic perspectives and disciplinary ghettos that subscribe to catastrophic deficit-oriented perspectives.

In order to counteract such a disciplinary dogmatism, it is important to foreground the hitherto subjugated knowledge base of the political, social and cultural dimensions of disability and SEN. To this end, it is imperative to adopt critical perspectives, as well as a pluralistic theoretical and analytical framework predicated on the values of individual respect and equality, along with the need to converge some of their mutually exclusive dimensions in more 'inclusive' ways enacted through appropriate policy reforms (Norwich, 2010). As we have already discussed in terms of pedagogical approaches, some aspects of special education knowledge base can still have some place in radically reformed, well-resourced mainstream schools in order to enrich teaching and learning, expand supportive networks and enhance professional expertise. By no means are the political dimensions of disability and SEN disassociated from the day to day institutional routines and practicalities that need to be collectively and concurrently enforced in order to enact inclusive education.

That said, special educational needs should be understood as significantly being the result of complex and interactive social processes that are contextually and historically grounded. As a corollary to this, a student's disabled identity is regarded as being 'a complex amalgam, an often-messy matrix of human and social pathology' (Slee, 2011: 122). Such an approach is not limited to theoretical and philosophical rhetoric, but also has implications for improving educational practice. Hollenweger (2008: 11) questions the credibility of deficit-based accounts in informing effective provision for students designated as having disabilities and/or special educational needs:

> There is broad consensus and overwhelming evidence that one-dimensional, categorical conceptualizations of disability as attributes of individuals are no longer helpful in understanding how to improve educational systems and educational services.

This perspective is indicative of the necessity to reconceptualize special education policy and practice and provide alternative analytical lenses though which to fully understand the complexity of disability and special educational needs.

Theorizing special education: a historical perspective

The historical link of special education with scientific and functional perspectives has consolidated and perpetuated an erroneous form of thinking that has distorted the political nature of disability and special educational needs (Barton, 1996). The influence of this kind of thinking is still prevalent and continues to influence, albeit more subtly, education policy and practice. In effect, notwithstanding current international rhetoric around inclusive education, ample evidence suggests that occasionally inclusion remains at the realm of rhetoric while detrimental special education practices of the past are perpetuated and skilfully reconfigured under the banner of inclusion (Norwich, 2000; Slee, 2001b; Graham and Jahnukainen, 2011).

Special education has been historically entangled in the ideologies of 'professionalism' and 'expertism' (Fulcher, 1999) whereby power relations have been constituted and regenerated through segregating policies and practices. Through the 'individualised gaze' of medicine and psychology, disabled people have been widely discriminated against and construed as 'Other' or negatively different (Barton, 1996: 32). These discourses have solely adopted an essentialist perspective and placed the deficit within individuals, thereby ignoring the socio-political relationship between individuals and their environment. This perspective relates to a particular view of scientific rationality and the nature of scientific investigation that precludes any non-scientific considerations and interpretations. This perspective, however, 'depoliticises' disability since it is regarded as a 'technical issue beyond the exercise of power' (Fulcher, 1999: 26).

Professionals, based on the so-called 'scientific' knowledge, construct powerful discourses that depoliticise disability (Tomlinson, 1982), and privilege one-dimensional perspectives of individual pathology and deficit by establishing 'able-bodiness' as a 'benchmark against which physical and intellectual "normality"' is judged (Barnes et al., 1999: 85). Slee (1996: 114), for example, characterizes Attention Deficit Disorder/ Attention Deficit Hyperactivity Disorder (ADD/ADHD) as a 'syndrome of spectacular administrative convenience' since individual explanations have become a rather 'sophisticated and pervasive' means of control. The proliferation of unequal power relations and their linguistic and material embodiments have been widely used to obscure and naturalize exclusionary and deficit-oriented practices,

The clinical discourses of medicine and psychology have been legitimized on the basis of a humanitarian perspective allegedly intended to 'protect people from the harsher realities of life and from ordinary school life' (Belanger 2001: 38). As a result, institutionalization and deficit-oriented assumptions have been legitimated by an ostensibly caring and humanitarian philosophy embodied in the charity discourse of disability that 'sat well with the medical discourse' (Fulcher, 1999: 28). Disabled people have been portrayed as being in need of help (Leewellyn, 1983), as objects of pity (Borsay, 1986) and examples of personal tragedy (Oliver, 1986) (cited in Fulcher 1999: 28). Thus, as Barton and Tomlinson (1981: 24) have suggested, although 'the rhetoric of needs is humanitarian, the practice is control and vested interests'.

The politics of special educational needs and disability

In order to unveil the interplays of multiple dynamics and unequal power relations impacting on the processes of categorization and selection on the basis of ability, the field of special educational needs has been radically re-authored and re-articulated through new theoretical and analytical tools. Moving beyond the functional and, hence, absolutistic and pseudo-scientific perspectives by which the field has been significantly influenced, the aim has been to deploy emancipatory 'scepticism' and construe 'liberating alternatives'

(Gutting, 1994: 3), so as to reconceptualize and offer fresh perspectives on the notions of 'disability' and 'special educational needs'. This in turn has opened up new possibilities capable of facilitating educational change and constructing inclusion (Thomas and Loxley, 2007).

Sociological theorizing in special education has the potential, as Tomlinson (1982: 24) propounds, to analyze and ultimately deconstruct the 'structures of power and the way power is legitimated . . .' through the institutional and ideological infrastructure of a particular socio-political system. In this sense, special education policy should be conceptualized and theorized within an interactive network of ideological and structural dynamics (Grace, 1991) whereby the notion of power is central. Bearing in mind that the knowledge base of special education has been primarily constituted by dominant 'regimes of truth' (Foucault, 1984a), central to the analysis of education policy should be the thorough examination of these 'regimes' along with the discursive practices that produce and sustain them within different socio-political and historical contexts. Disability should thus be significantly understood as a discursively construed social process, within a particular social context, and special education should be reconceptualized as a socially constructed category that emanates from and is constituted by unequal power relations, which are reified through the institutional structures of a particular socio-political system.

What follows is an attempt to theorize special education policymaking in terms of the multifaceted interplay of unequal power relations. In order to achieve this, it is important to draw on interrelated sociological insights. In particular, the following sections are given over to an exploration of the ways in which *postmodern and poststructural* sociological accounts have contributed to our understanding of the complex nature of disability and special educational needs. It needs noting that despite their significant contribution to understanding the compounded processes of special educational policymaking, these analyses have been criticized on a number of bases, something that will be discussed in the final section of this chapter.

Theorizing special education: a new perspective

Modernist ideas hold that the knowledge base of special education has been the result of scientific methods of inquiry that constitute a credible and solid foundation in order to generate more knowledge and devise effective diagnoses and interventions. Disability has been conceptualized as a medical phenomenon that could be treated and accommodated. These modernist ideas have been firmly rooted in Enlightenment predicated on the premise of 'science as Truth' and embodied in absolutistic and rational perspectives (meta-narratives) and binary, either/or considerations (e.g., wellness versus illness, ability versus disability) (Goodley and Rapley, 2002; Scully, 2002; Gallagher, 2006). The fixation with these ideas has rationalized the binary thought of 'normality' and 'abnormality' and engendered the individual and medical models of disability, which 'perceive and classify disability in terms of a meta-narrative of deviance, lack and tragedy, and assume it to be logically separate from and inferior to "normalcy"' (Corker and Shakespeare, 2002: 2).

Postmodernism denounces modernist ideas of scientific inquiry, and advocates a socially constructed view of knowledge (see next section). Knowledge about reality is rather subjective, while neutrality and objectivity are utopian concepts as things and meanings, facts and values cannot be disentangled and viewed as distinct entities. Monolithic and monodimensional considerations of a single, rational and binary theoretical frame of reference for interpreting the social world are superseded by anti-foundational, or in other words, non-deterministic views of social knowledge. Theory is informed by our values, experiences, culture, intention and choices (Gallagher, 2001), and is inevitably subjected to the complexity inscribed in human systems, which by no means can be described as closed or as being subjected to general laws (Rubinstein, 1986). In effect, theory should emanate from a political stance, and should encompass a holistic investigation of meaning, significance and the social and historical contexts (Thomas and Loxley, 2007) within which theories emerge and get reified. Context thus acquires a pre-eminent position and constitutes an indispensable element in any critical endeavour. Having said this, theories should be regarded as precarious and contingent conceptual constructs that are discursively constituted within an interactive framework of historical, social and political dynamics.

While acknowledging the precarious nature of theories devised, it is crucial to eclectically deploy 'specific inquiries into a multitude of specific structures and interactions . . .' (Dewey in Meiklejohn, 1996: 83, cited in Thomas and Loxley, 2007: 16) that will lead to the reconsideration of so called 'scientific' explanations upon which the sacred certitudes of special education thinking and practice have been predicated so far, and which emanated from a specific 'frame of reference'. Understandably, the choice of a particular theoretical frame of reference is contingent upon the 'historic languages of feelings, sentiments, imaginings, fancies, desires . . . ' (Oakeshott, 1989: 65, cited in Thomas and Loxley, 2007: 29) that are deeply rooted in our basic beliefs, values, assumptions and considerations (Lindsay and Thompson, 1997). From this perspective, it is of crucial importance to:

> survey the current thinking of theorizing and to identify the broad trends which characterize current thinking. These trends tell us something about ourselves: they tell us about the assumptions which we are coming to share, the values which are implicit or explicit in our work and the priorities which we are embodying in our theories. (Clark et al., 1998: 156)

Theorizing about special education should thus be primarily based on moral terms (Gallagher, 2001), as it is mutually defined by people and it also constitutes a subjective and contingent endeavour. Special education theory, in this respect, is subject to a plethora of alternative 'possible knowledges or optional descriptions' (Skrtic 1995: 45), with profound implications for social justice (Skrtic 1991, 1995), an issue that is central to the re-conceptualization of special education and the quest for an inclusive discourse.

Postmodern/poststructural theorizing and special education

The relative nature of the theories devised and their inadequacy in explaining the complexity of disability and special SEN, along with the contention 'that Disability Studies, particularly in Britain, have suffered from a theoretical deficit' (Corker and Shakespeare, 2002a: 1) (see Chapter 5), have given rise to postmodern and poststructural perspectives and insights in analyzing disability and SEN (Corbett, 1993; Skrtic, 1995; Corker and Shakespeare, 2002; Tremain, 2005). Overcoming any forms of either/or thinking, selective strands of the two (post-) movements can, borrowing Foucault's proposition, be taken as 'openings . . . where those who may be interested are invited to join in' for a cross-disciplinary and pluralistic inquiry (cited in Tyler 1997: 77) that can unveil the contextual social and cultural factors that are implicated in special education policy constitution and dissemination.

Postmodernism is defined in multiple of ways. The fluidity of the term is well recognized (Turner, 1990; Baert, 1998; Crotty, 1998) and reflects the essence of postmodernism, which eschews any form of binaries (Peters, 1999), as well as any conceptual and philosophical confinements, and embraces a multitude of paradigmatic voices (Skrtic, 1991, 1995). Selective strands of postmodernism can thus be used and combined beyond any lines of demarcation, according to the foci points of social analysis.

Postmodernism is based on the assumption that 'truth' emerges from a dialogical process among a variety of perspectives and, therefore, special education can be theorized by using a plethora of paradigmatic voices. According to Gellner (1992: 24):

> Postmodernism would seem to be rather clearly in favour of relativism, in as far as it is capable of clarity, and hostile to the idea of unique, exclusive, objective, external or transcendent truth. Truth is elusive, polymorphous, inward, subjective . . . (cited in Hartley, 1994: 232)

Postmodernism is 'antireductionist and pluralist' (Agger, 1991: 116) and 'commits itself to ambiguity, relativity, fragmentation, particularity and discontinuity' (Crotty, 1998: 185). Hence, it denounces the reliance in dichotomous and monodimensional considerations (e.g., normality versus abnormality), and extends its scope of analysis to an all-encompassing agenda. It is therefore of great value in the field of special and inclusive education for it makes us 'aware of and tolerant toward social differences, ambiguity and conflict' (Corker and Shakespeare, 2002: 5). Thus, understanding special education entails

> a shift toward more multiperspectival theorizing that respects a variety of sometimes conflicting perspectives rather than, as in modern theory, seeking the one standpoint of objective truth or absolute knowledge. (Best and Kellner, 2001: 113).

Hence, postmodern perspectives view disability as a socially constructed and contextually grounded phenomenon that results from negative connotations of difference emanating, for instance, from biomedical perspectives that ascribe to singular '"valid" embodiments – embodiments that can be referred to as the normal/healthy body' (Scully, 2002: 53). Special education knowledge is thus redefined and understood as being 'contextualised by its historical and cultural nature' (Agger, 1991: 117). Shakespeare and Watson (2001) draw on postmodern accounts in order to criticize modernist dichotomous perspectives that draw a clear demarcation line between 'impairment' and 'disability', between the 'personal' and 'the social'. They argue that a person's impairment is not biological but significantly social because, 'The words we use and the discourses we deploy to represent impairment are socially and culturally determined' (Shakespeare and Watson, 2001: 18). For instance, some disability categories, like 'learning disability' or 'dyslexia' are, according to Hollenweger (2008: 2), 'neither "true" not "real" without reference to the specific context in which they have emerged or were developed'. Goodley and Rapley (2002: 127) also utilize postmodern/poststructural insights in order to 'challenge both the modernist constructions of "learning difficulties" as naturalised impairment, and also demonstrate that phenomena frequently understood as being an essential feature of "intellectual disability" are better understood as aspects of social interaction'.

Along similar lines, Sailor and Paul (2004: 39) exemplify the importance of postmodern critique in transcending futile binaries and absolutistic considerations in special education research, which polarize the field and fail to address issues of 'voice', 'democracy', 'inclusion' and 'participation'.

> Postmodern criticism is relevant to the human services professions (i.e., special education) because it moves us beyond endless conflicts between, for example, experimental versus qualitative research paradigms and their relative contributions to structured interventions that will help children. Rather, a radically different form of discourse is proposed: one that is (a) inclusive and participatory, (b) incorporates the voice and perspectives of those affected by research conducted by scientist practitioners and other professionals, and (c) accepts or rejects theoretical perspectives on the basis of whether they contribute to the realization of democratic ideals, rather than whether they reflect a metaphysical foundation of knowledge . . .

In some cases postmodernism is perceived as being synonymous with poststructuralism, in spite of their differing theoretical antecedents (Agger, 1991; Peters, 1999). Their philosophical merging is not reprehensible as some of their theoretical standpoints either overlap or complement each other. They are both characterized by an 'aversion to clean positivist definitions and categories' (Agger, 1991: 112) that have historically dominated special education policy and practice through, for instance, the use of psychometric tests and systems of disability classification and categorization in education (Burk and Ruedel, 2008). In this respect, arbitrary and dogmatic templates of 'normality', against which the 'otherness' image of some individuals is constructed, need to be questioned and challenged, so as to foreground their precarious, contextual and ultimately political nature.

Poststructuralism, like postmodernism, rejects 'metaphysical dualisms' (Skrtic and Sailor, 1996: 274) that engender dichotomous perspectives on normality-abnormality, and challenges according to Peters (1999: 62):

> . . . . scientism in the human sciences, introduces an anti-foundationalism in epis-
> temology and a new emphasis upon perspectivism in interpretation. The move-
> ment challenges the rationalism and realism that structuralism continues from
> positivism, with its promethium faith in scientific method . . .

From this perspective, it is held that there is nothing inherently true in special education as is constituted by a plethora of 'paradigms' that emerge from the 'frame of reference' of the most powerful social actors. Knowledge becomes then indispensable from power, as they co-exist and are constantly implicated in a dynamic and reciprocal relation. Given this, knowledge ceases to be considered as a simple representation of reality, and as a corollary to this the various forms of scientific and rational thought are challenged (Peter and Humes, 2003).

For Foucault (1977a), the search for truth was not the result of a scientific enquiry per se, but the result of an unveiling process aimed at exposing the unequal power relations that constitute certain subjectivities (e.g., students with special educational needs). It was more or less a new-conceptualized historical inquiry whereby the gazes concentrated on the dynamic micro textures of discourse that constitute the prevalent 'regimes of truth' (Foucault, 1984a) that reside in and are disseminated by dominant institutions such as medicine, psychology and social work. Foucault understands the constitution of truth/knowledge as the result of complex networks of power that are inexorably linked with social economic and political factors. As he writes:

> We should admit rather that power produces knowledge . . . that power and
> knowledge directly imply one another; that there is no power relation without
> the correlative constitution of a field of knowledge, nor any knowledge that does
> not presuppose and constitute at the same time power relations . . . (Foucault,
> 1977a: 27)

Foucault attempts to provide a 'historicized ontology' (Peters, 1999, 2003) and concomitantly disqualifies ontology, which holds a rational respect for the facts of reality, as a sufficient theoretical construct for interpreting the social world. Hence, his work has been concerned with exploring the ways by which human beings are becoming objects of investigation, surveillance and treatment through social practices that legitimate forms of medicalization, incarceration and exclusion.

A distinctive feature of adopting a Foucauldian perspective to understand disability is the importance attributed to 'language' and 'symbolism' and 'power' in constructing disabled and hence subjugated identities (Hughes, 2005). As Corker and Shakespeare (2002: 8) write:

> A Foucauldian perspective on disability might argue, then, that a proliferation of discourses on impairment gave rise to a category of 'disability'. Though these discourses were originally scientific and medical classificatory devises, they subsequently gained currency in judicial and psychiatric fields of knowledge.

For instance, in the *Birth of the Clinic*, Foucault (1973) provides a genealogical analysis of the ascendancy and legitimization of the medical profession, which can be traced to the end of the eighteenth century when 'medicine acquires the clarity and power that is necessary to make disease (and by implication impairment) knowable' (Hughes, 2005: 82). In that way the binary perspectives between the 'normal' and the 'pathological' came into being and engendered 'the dualistic logic that legitimates the invalidation of people on the grounds of bodily difference from a medically fabricated norm and, furthermore, valorises a regime of truth in which impairment offends against the biological laws of nature' (ibid.).

During the nineteenth century, living phènoménes (humans with physical anomalies) were popular and highly attractive entertainers to spectators in Parisian streets, until the time they were imputed an 'abhorrent' and sub-human status that relegated them to the fringes of society. The advent of their abnormal status spread fear and subverted their subject positions as entertainers through their depiction as repulsive and deviant abnormal human beings, not 'fit' and 'normal' enough to be exposed to public view (Tremain, 2005). The advent of new knowledge like eugenics and social Darwinism relegated any kind of human difference to the sphere of 'abnormality' and 'social deviance'. As a result, 'difference' was equated with 'abnormality' that needed to be contained and controlled through an array of disciplinary and surveillance techniques (Snigurowicz, 2005; Tremain, 2005). Snigurowicz (2005) cites the example of Mille Brison, a 24-year-old woman with congenital malformation of the limbs, who in February 1906 was accused of violating the police ordinance that no longer allowed the exposure of living phènoménes in fairs and carnivals. The ascendancy and legitimization of binary perspectives of normality and abnormality ascribed any perceived lack of bodily integrity to social and criminal deviance that needed to be policed and investigated.

Medical professionals were then given ample credentials to adjudicate perceived deviations from physiological, psychological and cognitive 'norms' with a view to devising and prescribing remedies to approximate arbitrarily fabricated notions of 'normalcy'. It was at that time that disabled people's subject positions were significantly subordinated by rendering them objects of individualistic gaze and subjecting them to the exercise of power stemming from medical loci of control, allegedly intended to safeguard their best interests.

Given the emergence of new perspectives and alternative insights, special education categories should thus be seen as precarious historical and socio-political artefacts arbitrarily constituted by interplays of unequal power relations, and reified through the institutional arrangements of different socio-political contexts. Graham (2005) draws on poststructural perspectives in order to question the construction of 'disorderly' schooling identities in a particular socio-political system. The construction of these identities is based on a particular notion of normality that is understood as:

> a man-made grid of intelligibility that attributes value to culturally specific performances and, in doing so, privileges particular ways of being. . . . The norm derived from psychological knowledge works to construct the ab/normal binary from which we draw conclusions about the nature, characters and aptitudes of individual school children. (Graham, 2005: 5)

In a similar way, Danford and Rhodes (1997: 358) exemplify the role of deconstruction, as a form of poststructural critique, in problematizing and ultimately subverting the 'binary logic' that engenders 'moral and political categories based on "ability" and "disability"'. This line of thought highlights the role of 'words', 'actions' and 'ideas' in valorizing certain human attributes while rejecting and devaluing some others. It is thus suggested that:

> if our society (professional and nonprofessional realms) suddenly lost the vocabulary of mental retardation, somehow relinquishing terms such as intelligence, normal, disability, and so on, the constructed reality of mental retardation would no longer continue in its present form. New terms and concepts of description would emerge, because people seem to inevitably rely on schemes of categorization to explain the actions of individuals. Yet the change to new terms could be for the political and moral better, allowing those previously labelled persons to be viewed and treated in a more respectful way. (Danford and Rhodes, 1997: 361)

That said, oppressive and discriminatory policies and practices with regard to disability and special educational needs are understood as being the result of interplays of power that engender and impose dogmatic templates of normality and negative connotations of difference. As a corollary to this, special education policy and practice should be examined against a broader perspective beyond the confinements of what Slee (2001c: 117) has once described as 'a deep epistemological attachment to the view that special education needs are produced by the impaired pathology of the child'.

Postmodern/poststructural theorizing: A multi-paradigm shift and its implications for special education policy and practice

As earlier discussed, Foucault and his genealogy reject absolute and deterministic positions and give prominence to the relative nature of objects and practices which are dependent upon the context within which they arise (Foucault 1977b). While studying history, a genealogist:

> . . . finds that there is 'something altogether different' behind things: not a timeless and essential secret, but the secret that they have no essence or that their essence was fabricated in a piecemeal fashion from alien forms. (Foucault, 1977b: 142)

Genealogy, thus, opens up new possibilities to conceptualize and explicate the discourses of power and practice that influence and ultimately constitute the essence of special education policymaking. Similarly, Derrida (1976, 1979) applies the dialogical process to meaning in the sense that meaning is not within the words we use and, therefore, there is not a single meaning or interpretation within a theory or a philosophical system (Benton and Craib, 2001).

To this end, the debates should not focus on the nature of disability and whether disability is '*true* but how its objects *might become formed*; that is, how is this particular difference articulated and brought to attention and what might be the "effects in the real"' (Graham, 2005: 7). Arbitrary fabrications of normality have been used as legitimate heuristic devices to identify individuals with presumed 'abnormal' developmental trajectories and personal attributes, in order to relegate them to a 'descending order of human value' (Slee, 2006: 112).

In this respect, special education policy and practice can be conceived of as having been based on erroneous grounds, as the inadequacies of the education system have been merely attributed to individual pathology and school organization (Skrtic, 1991), without giving concomitant consideration to the social processes and the power struggles which are implicated in that process and which ultimately constitute the essence of special education. Hence, in order to look beyond the practices of special education we should consider the multiple 'realities' that constitute the complexity of special education, and provide a multidimensional and interactive framework of social analysis. It needs noting, however, that by doing this the aim is not to 'mask' or annihilate disability and individual needs. Rather, the aim is to uncover the socio-political dynamics that give rise to and multiply disabling and oppressive regimes. As Morris, a disabled writer and activist writes, '. . . our grief is not a failure to come to terms with disability. Our dissatisfaction with our lives is not a personality defect but a sane response to the oppression which we experience' (cited in Barton, 1993: 237).

Special education policy and practice should thus be regarded as the result of a plethora of paradigmatic voices vying for dominance within the wider socio-political context. Power is 'dispersed, not centralised in society' (Baert, 1998: 124), and thereby new meanings and new theorizations emerge from power struggles, which are disseminated and reside within all arenas of a political and educational system (Fulcher, 1999) and which ultimately construct 'knowledge'. By implication, the politics of disability should primarily be concerned with identifying and destabilizing disabling ideologies along with their institutional embodiments, which denounce anything that goes beyond the contours of a contested and arbitrary conception of normality.

Given the perplexity of the issues at hand, the debate about special education should thus be placed in a much wider context and encompass a thorough critique of micro and macro dynamics which undermine the attempts towards transformative change. Post-functional theorizing embraces the utilization of other accounts for interpreting the social world that enable the researcher to move beyond the 'tidy generalities' of policy studies, and acknowledge and pursue its 'messy realities' (Ball, 1990: 9). That said, sociological accounts have also been based on structural perspectives, which lend support to the fact that conflict is endemic in special education. Structural and conflict theories have been used extensively in studying social institutions and processes, whereby special education is not an exception, and are primarily represented by the works of Marx and Weber (Tomlinson, 1982). An example of the conflict that is inherent in special education is manifested in the contradictory policies that exist and pose discursive confinements, as well as confound education policy. Ware (2002: 144) points to the fact that '[e]ducation's twin goals of efficiency and equity have proven increasingly paradoxical and antithetical to inclusion, yet the system's pathology continues to be recast as student pathology'.

Similarly, Wedell (2005: 2) talks about the inconsequent and contradictory character of national policies, whereby 'national education policies often act to frustrate each other in their implementation', and defines this as an example of system problems. As we have seen, on the one hand policies are concerned with social justice and equality of opportunity and on the other hand the marketization of education has increasingly become a dominant policy imperative (Taylor, 2004). In consequence, education policy documents are riddled with what Slee (1996a) calls 'clauses of conditionality' whereby the right of disabled students to be educated in their neighbourhood mainstream school is concomitantly disenfranchised by provisional and contingent statements resulting from unequal power relations. Institutionally empowered social actors 'hide behind the clauses of conditionality (Slee, 1996) in the legislation to provide forms of segregation' (Slee, 2001a: 389). The discretionary power statutorily assigned to them can legitimately construct 'need' and 'deficit' and unobtrusively debar disabled students from mainstream schools.

The synthesis of diverse theoretical standpoints has the potential to deconstruct special education and bring to the surface the relativity and fluidity of the term. Central to the synthesis of approaches is the recognition that the revelation and thorough investigation of the dominant 'frame of reference' within which the various discourses (the material effects of language-use) underpinning special education policy are formed and reified have significant political and moral implications for both individuals and societies (Barton, 1993; Skrtic, 1995).

If we are to proceed to educational change and construct inclusion, we need to illuminate the ways that power manifests itself, thus exposing as Peters and Humes (2003: 112) suggest, the 'structures of domination by diagnosing "power/knowledge" relations and their manifestations in the classifications, typologies and institutions'. Put differently, we should reveal and critique the dominant discourses that both implicitly and explicitly steer and eventually shape special education policy. As Slee (2011: 126) writes:

> The more pervasive the knowledge and authority of the constitution of normality, and the more precise we make our calibration and cartography of deviations from those norms, then the greater is our disciplinary power and ability to assert governance over complex populations.

Of crucial importance, therefore, is to acknowledge the necessity to question the representations and subject positions of disabled people as these are constructed and disseminated by powerful social actors through special education policy. Quoting Foucault (1980c: 117) once more: 'One has to dispense with the constituted subject, to get rid of the subject itself . . . to arrive at an analysis which can account for the constitution of subject within a historical framework . . . '

This relativistic and historicized perspective on social reality highlights the inherent arbitrariness in positioning certain subjectivities as 'abnormal' and 'deviant', thereby providing a fertile and liberating ground for debate and critique. Central to this endeavour is to disentangle and interrogate the convoluted relationships between ideologies, discourses and unequal power relations underpinning the policymaking process with regard to disability and special educational needs. The question then, is to devise and explicate a pluralistic 'frame of reference', upon which special education policy analysis will be based.

Just like Foucault's problematizations and histories that never stop, the subtleties of the sought frame of reference for education policy analysis should be constantly interrogated and reformed in order to encapsulate and portray the contextualized and historicized conditions against which the 'politics of disability and special educational needs' are played out and acted upon in the policymaking process.

Reflective Exercise

What is the role of power in understanding and analyzing the notion of special educational needs?

Theoretical pluralism under scrutiny: implications for political action

Despite acknowledging the need for adopting a pluralistic theoretical framework of analysis in order to fully understand the complex and contested nature of disability and special educational needs, Barton (1997: 240) alerts us to the necessity of avoiding postmodern analyses leading to a 'political cul-de-sac which, in relation to groups of individuals who are excluded and oppressed, becomes part of a disabling discourse'. This can be attributed to the occasionally 'obscure' and 'opaque' character of the language underpinning postmodern and poststructural theorizing, an issue that by itself constitutes a disabling discourse. Moreover, another significant issue of concern is the extent to which these accounts have any impact on the 'struggle to end the oppression of disabled people' and mobilize attempts for transformative change (Corker and Shakespeare, 2002: 14). Oliver and Barton (2000: 8) are also sceptical over the ways in which some sociological accounts have 'immediate relevance to the struggles of disabled people to lead a decent life'.

Thus, notwithstanding, for instance, the significant contribution of Foucauldian analyses to disability studies, there has been criticism over Foucault's one-dimensional conception of power that undermines disability politics. It is suggested that Foucauldian analyses of the power knowledge grid might lead to what Hughes (2005: 90) calls 'a cul-de- sac that forecloses access to an emancipatory conception of power'. The emancipatory conception of power mobilizes political agency embodied in the role of grassroots activism and other social movements around rights and equality, so as achieve transformative change and 'create spaces for new knowledge and forms of action to emerge . . . ' (Barton, 2001: 5). Quoting Hughes (2005: 90): 'If power is reduced to structures of domination, it is not logical for impaired [sic] people to contest disablism. Only fatalism makes sense'. Hence, without the emancipatory conception of power, disabled people 'might as well lie down to the discrimination and exclusion that disables their lives. If power is "panoptic" and in eliminable, then disability politics is inconceivable' (Hughes, 2005: 90).

Emancipatory change necessitates, according to Barton (1997: 240), going 'beyond flirtations with postmodernism and urgently begin to address the challenges of developing an adequate theory of political agency' Political agency can be facilitated, for instance, by devising emancipatory and participatory research agendas that take into consideration the voices of disabled people in order to precipitate fundamental social and educational change. As Barton (2005: 319) writes:

> In a culture of domination, power relations are a means of silencing particular voices, thus within such a historical and cultural context finding a voice is an essential part of the struggle for freedom.

Nevertheless, despite the above considerations, it needs noting that in his later writings Foucault also conceptualizes the emancipatory potentials of power and the '"strategic reversibility" of power relations' (Foucault, 1991: 5). As Foucault (1980: 13) writes:

> I'm not positing a substance of power. I'm simply saying: as soon as there's a relation of power there's a possibility of resistance. We're never trapped by power: It's always possible to modify its hold, in determined conditions and following a precise strategy.

Thus, the relations of power are not always confined to the subjugating effects of power, but they imply the productive effects of power, something that spawns possibilities of resistance and reversibility. These possibilities flare an air of optimism and make transparent that the nexus of knowledge and power that give rise to disabling discourses, policies and practices can be dismantled and subverted if, however, this is pursued in consistent and politically informed ways.

Summary

This chapter has provided an alternative voice to the scientific explanations upon which special education policy and practice have been traditionally based. The aim has been to question the conceptual status quo that has traditionally held sway over the field and discriminated against disabled people and their advocates. Postmodern/poststructural accounts can contribute to providing an enlightened theory of special education that envisages questioning of individual pathology imperatives. The pluralistic character of this kind of theorization challenges the confinements of functional thought and seeks to bring to the surface the power/knowledge grid that undermines attempts towards transformative change.

Theorizing about special education should be regarded as being an ever-changing and unending process, which by no means should be considered prescriptive or permanent, and it should not distract attention from other crucial considerations and concerns for change, which should primarily characterize special education (Thomas and Loxley, 2007). What we should ultimately bear in mind is the necessity to humanize special education, thus acknowledging its contingent and provisional nature.

The next chapter is concerned with the complicated nature of inclusive education policymaking, which is constituted within an interactive framework of unequal power relations. Inclusive education policy analysis seeks to bring to the surface the plethora of dynamics, stemming both from actors and structures that influence the ways in which inclusion is conceptualized and acted upon. This is an important task, if we are to understand the reasons as to why the road towards the realization of an inclusive discourse has been an extremely 'difficult and disturbing task' (Barton, 1997: 232).

Reflective Exercise

In what alternative ways can the notion of 'special educational needs' be understood and analyzed?

What is the significance of post-functional theorizing in understanding the complexity of special educational needs and disability?

Useful websites

Centre for Disability Studies
    www.leeds.ac.uk/disability-studies
The Disability Archive UK
    www.leeds.ac.uk/disability-studies/archiveuk/
Interdisciplinary Disability Research Institute
    www.idris.ac.uk
UNEnable-Work of the United Nations for Persons with Disabilities
    www.un.org/disabilities/
Independent Living Institute
    www.independentliving.org/

4

Understanding Inclusive
Education Policymaking

Chapter Outline

Introduction

In this chapter the aim will be to explain the complicated nature of inclusive educational policymaking as it is constituted within an interactive network of reciprocal and adversarial relations. Within this context, policies are understood as being '. . . instruments of power/knowledge relations through which the identities and experiences of children with special educational needs are constructed' (Slee, 2001: 389). It is no coincidence, then, that the attempts for the realization of an inclusive discourse have been characterized as a struggle (Vlachou, 1997), and in particular, as a discursive struggle whereby a profusion of interrelated social, historical, ideological dynamics influence the processes and outcomes of the policymaking process. It is crucial that the critical examination and analysis of these dynamics should be brought to the centre rather than the periphery of educational policy analysis.

In particular, the chapter provides a comprehensive and all-encompassing definition of inclusive education policymaking by making transparent the ever changing realities influencing the policymaking process over time and space, and identifying the diverse and contradictory values and beliefs vying for ascendancy (Fulcher, 1999) and influencing official education policy landscapes pertaining to inclusion. Ultimately, then, the aim will be to offer a comprehensive account of the conceptualization of educational policy, along with some interpretations of the various parameters that shape education policy and have an impact on the translation of policy into practice. This is fundamental to the attempts to understand the ways in which an assemblage of dynamics are at play and bring to bear a profound impact on the ways in which the education of disabled children is envisaged and enacted.

Complexity is the trademark of social sciences, and inclusive education policymaking does not constitute an exception. The quest for inclusive education is anchored in this complexity and, hence, the realization of the former becomes a painstaking and contested endeavour. The processes and outcomes of educational policymaking are by no means a matter of serendipity (Ball, 1994). Rather, they are the result of a prodigious and difficult-to-depict discursive struggle between adversary and contradictory dynamics emanating from different 'loci' of power within a particular socio-political and historical context (Fulcher, 1999). The highly political nature of inclusion necessitates exploring the variegated macro (institutional, economic) and micro (ideological) dynamics impacting the processes and outcomes of educational policymaking, in order to fully understand the reasons as to why inclusion is a highly complex and contested pursuit.

Education policymaking is thus defined as being a political struggle (Fulcher, 1999) implicated in a multidimensional and interactive network – comprised both by structures and actors. A constitutive element of this interactive network is the notion of ideology, which, if examined from a critical perspective (Chapter 5), is directly implicated in the interplay of unequal power relations emanating both from human agency and structures.

Policies do not exist in an ideological vacuum as they reflect and embody 'underlying ideologies and assumptions in a society' (Armstrong et al., 2000: 7). These ideologies and assumptions are so deep-rooted in social consciousness that they occasionally become naturalized and are considered as facts. The dominant ideologies emerge from incessant and multilayered struggles within diverse political arenas throughout the educational apparatuses (Fulcher, 1999). These struggles are defined by Lindblom (1959, 1977) as 'a hard bargaining' amongst competing social actors with differing objectives and unequal power relations (cited in Drake, 1999: 23). In a similar vein, Gale (2001: 389–90) utilizes Foucault's genealogy as a means to explore the subtleties of the policymaking process, along with the ways in which 'alliances are formed and reformed around conflicting interests in the policy production process'.

Education policy is part of wider social policy and the welfare state in general. Consequently, education policy is interlinked and develops in parallel with other initiatives in social policy (Oliver, 1988). By implication, inclusive education policymaking should be viewed in relation to wider economic and social interests of a developing society (Barton and Armstrong, 2001) that determine the ways in which disability and special educational needs are conceptualized and defined. As Barton and Tomlinson (1984: 65) have argued, special education is a 'product of complex social, economic and political considerations which may relate more to the "needs" of the wider society, the whole education system and the professionals within the system, rather than simply to the "needs" of individual children'.

Education policy analysis seeks to foreground the unequal power relations emanating both from actors and structures, and expose the dominant discourses impacting upon inclusive education policy formulation and implementation (Ball, 1990; Ozga, 1990). In so doing it will be possible to gain some insight into the power struggles that are at play and influence the ways in which the education and life trajectories of disabled children are conjured up and acted upon.

Inclusive education policy analysis

Education policy analysis pertaining to inclusion is essential in order to examine the interplay of unequal power relations and critically analyze the nature of discourses underpinning the processes and outcomes of a particular policy. This is an important task in the pursuit of a radical human rights approach to inclusive education policy and practice (Barton and Armstrong, 2007). According to Berkhout and Wielemans (1999: 407):

> Policy analysis must be committed to the critical analysis of values in current policies as part of the process of clarifying the values that the analyst believes should inform both educational and public policy.

Emerging political exigencies and socio-historical conjunctures shape and reshape national education policy landscapes. Different governments, aligned with particular parties and political orientations, usually uphold different perspectives and ideologies that can potentially reshape the education policy landscape. It is usually the case that educational policies are substantially revised when new ideological and socio-political dynamics emerge. As Cross and Moses (1994: 281) write, whilst exploring the processes of educational policy genesis and implementation:

> Policy issues in Western democratic political systems are typically dominated by political partisanship. Policies are usually associated with a party or coalition of parties, and are usually disputed with opposing parties.

For instance, the advent of the New Right ideology (see Chapter 5), a strand of which is neo-liberalism, has brought to bear a significant impact on education policymaking in Western countries, with a notable example the case of the United Kingdom (Quicke, 1988). The aims of education have been significantly subsumed within the wider neo-liberal concerns of the state (freedom of choice, the individual and the market), something that is also manifested in current versions of inclusion as discussed in Chapter 1. In this respect, issues of human rights, equity and social justice are subordinated to the demands of the neo-liberal discourse of intense competition and meritocracy (Barton and Slee, 1999; Bottery, 2000).

Much debate has also taken place over the viability of certain accounts for educational policy analysis (e.g., Ozga, 1987, 1990; Ball, 1990) that have a direct impact on the ways in which inclusion has been conceptualized and enacted upon by social actors (Allan, 2005; Lingard and Mills, 2007). These accounts have ranged from Marxist to pluralistic accounts, whereby most of them have been prone to futile binaries, despite the complexity of issues at hand. Such forms of binaries act, according to Hargreaves (1983), as a hindrance for the development of education policy terrain (cited in Ozga, 1987). Consequently, the various strands of these hitherto divergent dimensions of a futile binarism need to be explicated and brought into a convergent framework for the analysis of education policy (Ranson, 1995).

Ozga (1990: 359) asserts that it is crucial to 'bring together structural, macro level analyses of education systems and education policies and micro level investigation, especially that which takes account of people's perceptions and experiences'. This convergent conceptual framework has the potential to delineate the multiple and reciprocal relations between values and materials, which beget policy 'contextualization' and 'recontextualization' (Ball, 1994; 2008). Ultimately, then, it will be possible to offer a multilevel historical and sociological account of the conceptualization of educational policy, along with some interpretations of the various parameters that shape education policy and have impact on the translation of policy into practice.

It needs noting, however, that policy analysis is pursued by a vantage point and constitutes a subjective endeavour that is contingent on interpretation (Taylor, 1997; Gale, 2001). Policy is itself a contested term, there is no fixed or a single definition of it, and as Ozga (2000: 2) writes, how the term is 'understood depends to a considerable degree on the perspective of the researcher' and the way she/he considers and examines the ever-changing influences and ideologies that lie behind policies. In much the same way, Danzinger (1995) discusses the political nature of policy analysis and the inevitable immersion of the analyst in the political process. Nevertheless, despite these scepticisms, the adoption of a certain mode of analysis does not constitute an arbitrary conceptual construct. Rather, it is predicated on a comprehensive socio-historical account that provides the backdrop against which the chosen mode of analysis is placed and explicated.

The conceptualization of educational policy as a linear process of policy formulation and implementation, within a 'state control' model of education, has been increasingly challenged and replaced by a more complex and dialectical process (Ball and Bowe, 1992; Fulcher, 1999). Education policy analysis thus becomes a multifaceted and, hence, demanding process that seeks to examine a wide range of complementary, adversary and interactive elements that constitute the complexity of educational policymaking processes within the consecutive cycles of policy 'formulation', 'recontextualization' and 'implementation' (Ball and Bowe, 1992).

In order to achieve an integrated approach to educational policymaking analysis (Berkhout and Wielemans, 1999), it is important to examine the different contexts in policy analysis and to establish and explicate possible interconnections or inconsistencies, not only within the contexts but also between these contexts. Binarism, in this sense, acts merely as an analytical tool, which investigates the parts of the whole before proceeding to the 'bigger picture' (Grace, 2001) of education policy, within which any lines of demarcation and, hence, any kinds of binarism are annihilated. In this respect, the aim is to go beyond 'analysis' and proceed to the synthesis of parts, so as to establish 'contextual relations' (Grace, 1991) through a 'toolbox of diverse concepts and theories' (Ball, 1993; 1994b). In so doing, it will be possible to achieve what Grace (1991: 3) calls 'policy scholarship' as opposed to 'policy science' that 'is seductive in its concreteness, its apparently value free and objective stance, and its relation to action'. This kind of holistic and critical approach to policy analysis can better illuminate, quoting Berkhout and Wielemans (1999: 404), the:

> powerful interactive force of networks and/or other structures and actors in a world of pluralistic policy-making. A focus on the formal or official state mechanisms of the education policy process negates the hidden, covert, informal, or implicit dimensions where power is exercised more unobtrusively.

This is particularly important in inclusive education policy analysis whereby the notion of power is central in exploring the ways in which disabling discourses and procedures are (re)generated and acted upon in every arena of a socio-political system. Understanding inclusive education involves a concomitant understanding of exclusion along with the ways in which it is masked through more inclusive veneers (Slee, 2011).

Bowe et al. (1992) refer to the three contexts of policy and discuss the contradictory considerations and complexities they might entail. The different contexts are referred to as the 'context of influence', the 'context of policy text production' and the 'context of practice'. Policymaking cycles are conceptualized by Berkhout and Wielemans (1999: 417) as 'differentiated', 'interrelated' and 'dynamic' societal fields or contexts that are variously implicated in the policymaking process.

The 'context of influence' is where the intended policy is constituted in the sense that it is within this context that policy discourses are inaugurated. Within the 'context of influence', according to Bowe et al. (1992: 20), 'key policy concepts are established (e.g., market forces, National Curriculum, opting out, budgetary devolution), they acquire currency and credence and provide a discourse and lexicon for policy initiation'. The powerful interested groups within the governmental terrain attempt to 'articulate' and 'impose' their own policy discourses, which are also influenced by what is happening in the other sectors of the government or internationally. These discourses are influenced by ideologies, interests, aspirations, political exigencies and historical conjunctures, and constitute the powerful discourses through which educational policymaking is contested and eventually contextualized within and across the 'policymaking cycles' (Ball and Bowe, 1992).

The 'context of influence', is profoundly affected by supranational organizations like the United Nations, the European Union, the Organization for African Unity, the International Monetary Fund and the World Bank (Berkhout and Wielemans, 1999: 417). Vongalis-Macrow (2005) discusses the role of global agencies in shaping education policies and explores the tensions, paradoxes and politics that ensue when these agencies promulgate contradictory responses to globalization, something that has serious repercussions for education policy and practice. She cites the examples of UNESCO and the World Bank whose role is significant in shaping educational policy and practice. As she writes:

> Current education policy from the mid 1990s onwards highlights the role of globally orientated organizations to increasingly incorporate education as part of the ongoing economic development agenda in the global era. . . . How the global agencies steer reforms suggests underlying tensions around responses to globalisation, partly due to disagreement over how globalisation is constructed. When UNESCO policy specifically takes an anti-neoliberal stance, implications are that other agencies are neo-liberal in their policy. Thus, UNESCO advocates 'real' democracy that accounts for social and cultural differences while World Bank discourse is grounded in the language of neo-liberal efficiency criteria. (Vongalis-Macrow, 2005: 6–9)

UNESCO's concerns for 'real democracy' are, for instance, manifested in the Salamanca Statement that sanctions the statutory duties of nation states in recognizing the right of disabled children to be educated alongside their peers in mainstream settings, or more recently, the Human Rights Action Plan (see Chapter 1). These initiatives have significantly influenced the introduction of antidiscrimination legislation and legislative mandates promoting inclusion in different geopolitical jurisdictions across the world. On the other hand, neo-liberal influences exerted by certain supranational bodies (e.g., World Bank), might be counterproductive in fostering greater inclusive policies and practices, taking as an example the ways in which neo-liberal ideologies (see Chapter 5) emanating from global capital put pressure on nation states in order to become more competitive, something that has significant implications for the ways in which the role of education is defined and acted upon.

Within the remit of the 'context of influence', Berkhout and Wielemans (1999: 417) also refer to 'the numerous other societal subsystems interacting with the education system (e.g., economic changes and labor market conditions and political-ideological contestations)'. Within this context they identify the role that indigenous religion and ideologies play in inclusive education policy constitution and dissemination within different socio-political contexts.

Whilst one might expect that the 'context of text production' is the direct result of the 'context of influence', this is not the case. The two contexts have, as Bowe et al. (1992: 20) contend, a 'symbiotic but an uneasy relationship'. Ideological dynamics and influences are not being magically 'converted' into formal policy as they entail contradictions and inconsistencies, which beget contestations over contestations and so forth. As Levin (1998: 134) contends, 'Most peoples' and all political systems' belief systems embody a range of ideas, all firmly held, but only some of which will be acted upon depending on circumstances'.

Thus, whatever the 'context of influence' might be, the 'context of text production' is usually geared towards the public good, which the State should provide whilst denouncing the 'dogmatic ideologies and narrow interests' embedded in the initial context (Bowe et al., 1992: 20). This is, however, an arduous and in some respects an elusive endeavour, as the existence of equal or more powerful policies upholding diametric antithetical agendas undermine such endeavours. As Ball (1994b: 16) so succinctly puts it, education policies are

> typically the cannibalised products of multiple (but circumscribed) influences and agendas. There is an ad hocery negotiation and serendipity within the state, within the policy formulation process.

In consequence, the State fails to maintain a balance between its espoused declarations and the social conflict inherent in policy constitution, and as a corollary to this policy implementation is confounded (Marshall and Patterson, 2002). Ball (1994c: 108) contends that 'we should not always expect to find policy coherence and should not be surprised to see struggle within the State over the definition and purpose of policy solutions'.

From a discourse perspective, whereby language is recognized as a potent source of social power, policymaking is regarded as being implicated within the 'politics of discourse' (Yeatman, 1999), whereby different discourses compete for ascendancy (cited in Fulcher, 1999). In this respect, policymaking is inevitably denoted by 'asymmetrical power relations' (Thompson, 1984) that determine both the formal and informal facets of educational policymaking. The dominance of the discourse of 'normalization' and 'the rule of homogeneity' along with the construction of 'hierarchies, hyponimic relations' (Foucault, 1979: 183, cited in Luke, 1996: 36) lead to the iniquitous demotion, or even 'disappearance', of disabled children's 'subject positions'. Hence, it is important to examine the nature of discourses which inform a particular policy and investigate the ways in which the 'gaze of authority, discipline and power marks out the same children as different, as deficit, as objects of the official knowledges and human silences of policing, education and welfare' (Luke, 1996: 36).

For instance, in trying to explore the 'subjectifying role' of education policies and document the extent to which 'a child is viewed as a person', Howie (2010: 761) notes that

> the British welfare legislation enacted later, has some acknowledgement of the person status generally, but when discussing persons with disabilities reverts to an objectification of the person. . . . The Special Educational Needs and Disability Act 2001 illustrates a lack of clear reference to the child's voice and continuing objectification of the child, with the requirements to 'inform the child's parent' even when the child is a pupil within a referral unit, concerning the provisions being made, assessment, etc. Only a parent may make a representation, and have the right to appeal. (Howie 2010: 761–3)

Another important issue that needs to be subjected to critical analysis is the way in which the contradictory and ambivalent nature of policies is manifested within the policies themselves and it is occasionally the case that the texts, which are the 'actual' policies, are riddled with contradictions and generalities, are occasionally vague and, in many instances, idealized. For instance, Young and Minz (2008: 501) whilst discussing the Individuals with Disabilities Education Act (IDEA) in the United States of America, write that despite its commitment to provide educational services to students in the 'least restrictive appropriate environment' the federal legislation gives space for providing a 'continuum of placement options which legally protects the ability of school districts to sustain segregated and restrictive classroom settings for students with disabilities through its broad interpretation'.

These legislative texts are characterized by an 'ideological impurity' (Norwich, 1996), or in other words, by 'discursive multiplicity' (Taylor, 2004: 434), in the sense that several contradictory discourses co-exist and are in tension. In effect, texts can be interpreted in varied ways within the 'context of practice' whereby policy is implemented by educational practitioners. In this respect, educational policy may be seen as an incessant succession of 'crises' and 'settlements' whereby the ideas of conflict and struggle are endemic to the policymaking process.

The 'context of text production' can be, in a way, characterized as the settlement whereby the divergent ideologies, interests and power relations come in a balanced assemblage, albeit a precarious one. Within the period of settlement, educational policy is imbued by certain principles which steer the educational system, in the sense that they provide the broader policy framework within which pursuant struggles will take place. The apparent stability of the policy settlement stage, however, will be challenged as soon as new socio-political, educational and economic agendas ascend and influence the policymaking process.

The ascendancy of new policy agendas is the result of political exigencies, partly emanating from influential international imperatives that necessitate the re-appraisal and modification of national policy landscapes. Foucault's genealogy and the concept of emergence capture the changeable and inconsistent nature of policy, which by no means can be characterized as a mere result of historical development. Rather, it can be characterized 'as a stage in the warlike confrontation between opposing forces in the quest for control and domination' (Marshall, 1990: 19).

Pre-eminent consideration should thus be given to the ever-changing role that ideology, politics, economics and interest groups play in the formation and implementation process (Grace, 1991). Accordingly, Ozga (2000: 114) contends that:

> Education policy is not confined to the formal relationships and processes of government, not only to schools and teachers, and to legislation affecting them. The broad definition requires that we understand it in its political, social and economic contexts, so that they also require study because of the ways in which they shape education policy . . . One way of approaching this is to look at the history of education policy making and its accompanying narrative of explanation of education policy that is provided by policy research.

This being the case, it can be held that education policy analysis cannot be limited to a specific parameter as might happen in other areas of social analysis. The 'specific' in policy analysis is primarily concerned with the subtle and varied interactions of the various parameters within the broader framework. The bigger picture (Grace, 1991) of educational policy analysis is an aggregation of its constituent parts within an interactive and reciprocally related network of power relations. There seems little doubt that any kind of monodimensional analysis fails to provide as Ball (1994b: 10) contends 'a decent theory of education policy'.

Even though the 'context of influence' does not coincide with the 'context of text production', it is within this context that the 'context of text production' emerges. The 'context of influence' encompasses a powerful and pervasive

discourse, which, albeit not relayed in its original state, is immensely influential and inevitably submerges, overtly or covertly, the context of text production. Powerful discourses do not emerge only from social actors, but also
from the institutional conditions through which discourses are regenerated,
bolstered and transformed. Relations of power are, as Foucault (1981: 94) contends, productive and they are not 'in a position of exteriority with respect to
other types of relationships (economic processes, knowledge relationships . . .)
but are immanent in the latter' (cited in Ball, 1994b: 20). Policy analysis, in this
sense, presupposes an in depth investigation of the ways in which power circu-
lates and 'is embedded/ embodied in every aspect, agent and agency involved
in the policy process' (Evans, 1994: 59). Particular emphasis should also be
placed on the ways that institutions promote, sustain or obliterate certain discourses and how these discourses are contested and reconstituted within institutions. Ultimately, it is through institutions that the most powerful actors
can relay their constructed knowledge, and exert in unobtrusive ways their
discourse, which is powerful only because it might be institutionally sanctioned. Anderson (1990: 40) articulates a critical approach to policy analysis
that seeks a 'better understanding of the often invisible ways in which social
interaction is "structured", power wielded, and privileged interests protected
in the organizational context'. This is especially true for special and inclusive
education, where the hegemonic role of professionals in exerting control over
disabled individuals and safeguarding their professional interests has been
widely discussed and critiqued (Tomlinson, 1982; Fulcher, 1999).

Having pursued an understanding of the processes inherent in the institutional conditions or structures, policy analysis also entails establishing interactive relations and consequential effects within the interplay of actors and
structures, namely the reciprocal and multiple interactions amongst ideologies, politics, interests and other historical conjunctures, as well as economics and institutional structures. This investigation should also extend to the
'context of practice', which is affected and framed, albeit not determined, by
the two other contexts. The 'context of practice' is a distinct arena, whereby
beyond the hegemonic knowledge that is inevitably relayed from the other
two contexts, it entails its own hegemonic knowledge, which results in a new
cycle of 'policy making'. To Bowe et al. (1992), schools are sites of contesta-
tion and politics and, hence, 'policy recontextualization', whereby policy is
not only implemented but also is '"recreated", not so much "reproduced" as
"produced"'. In this respect, educational practitioners are regarded as being
important policymakers within their contexts of practice whereby they have

the discretionary power to translate official policy into practice according to their beliefs, expectations and contextual realities (Fulcher, 1999).

The politics of inclusive educational policymaking

As already discussed, in order to understand the complexities and the difficulties endemic to the attempts to promote greater inclusive policies and practices, it is important to understand the nature of educational policymaking. Very simplistically, we tend to say that there is a gap between policy and practice without really thinking through and explicating the reasons as to why this gap has been created and what it means (Fulcher, 1999). Policy rhetoric does not magically translate into educational practice because educational policy in contemporary and dynamic socio-political systems is a rather complex, contingent and, hence, problematic issue (Berkout and Wielemas, 1999). As Marshall and Patterson (2002: 352) suggest, 'Policy implementation would be simple if stakeholders and educators agreed on values and whether the structures and resources were available. But these conditions will never exist in dynamic policy systems such as education.'

Hence, the policy development process is riddled with several contradictory considerations that are contingent upon the relationships between education, politics and the economy. In many instances, policies pertaining to the same 'agendas', promote inherently incompatible aims and perspectives as 'competing discourses are "stitched together"' (Taylor, 1995; 9 cited in Ball, 1998: 126) and confound educational policy implementation (Marshall and Patterson, 2002). Education policy should, therefore, be conceptualized and explained in terms of the 'changing ideological, economic and political parameters of policy' and 'relate the ideological, political and economic to the dynamics of policy debate and policy formulation' (Ball, 1990: 9).

This is a multifaceted and, hence, demanding process that seeks to examine the multitude of complementary, adversary and interactive elements that constitute the complexity of the educational policymaking process within the consecutive cycles of policy formulation, recontextualization and implementation (Ball and Bowe, 1992). Thus, whilst aiming at pursuing a comprehensive analysis of educational policymaking process, it is important to disentangle and examine these constitutive elements within the 'policymaking cycles' and discern all these instances whereby the 'loci of power' are constantly shifting (Bowe et al., 1992) in complex and interactive ways.

Central to education policymaking analysis should be the disentanglement and interrogation of the convoluted relationships between ideologies, discourses and unequal power relations immanent in the policymaking process. Although the concepts of ideology and discourse have been juxtaposed for their distinct theoretical antecedents, they can be constructively used by 'employing ideological analysis to focus upon the effects of discursive practices, which we term "ideology effects"' (Purvis and Hunt, 1993: 473). The focus should thus be placed on the ever-changing and contradictory discursive realities underpinning the policymaking process. The antithetical discourses are in a constant and intense tension for dominance and, as a result, educational policymaking becomes an arduous and complex process.

In this respect, Fulcher (1999), based on Hindess's theorization of educational policy, proposes a model whereby all practices are inherently political as they are based upon theoretical, political and moral discourses which are informed by hierarchical value-systems which are firmly embedded, as Demaine points out (1981: 13), in a 'range of arenas of political struggle where educational policy is debated and decisions made' (cited in Fulcher, 1986: 14). Within these arenas most policies are 'reworked, tinkered with, nuanced and inflected through complex processes of influence, text production, dissemination and, ultimately, recreation in context of practice' (Ball, 1998: 126). Thus, within the various formal or informal arenas, the various social actors (Hindess, 1986) make their own decisions and adopt a determinate stance towards educational issues.

From this point of view, educational reform is to a great extent the result of the resolutions and activities of the most powerful social actors who exert power and impose their own conceptual frameworks, desires and aspirations within all arenas of the educational apparatus, which in turn, have the potential to restructure and construe new social, political and economic realities. It is in this respect that advocates of change should put great emphasis on those domains, as David and Greene (1983: 134) put it, that are related with the people and their roles rather than materials or structures. In spite of the fact that social actors are to some extent subject to structures, they are regarded as being 'over and above' them. Therefore, given the incentives and the favourable conditions, social actors are able to alter the structural bases of the status quo and introduce change.

However, notwithstanding the significant role of social actors as a 'locus of control' (Baert, 1998), social life is not as Hindess (1986: 115) asserts reducible to 'the constitutive action of actors'. Thus, structural limitation impacts on educational policies and practices in more subtle ways, since the concept of 'determination' is replaced by that of 'delimitation' (Ball, 1990). In this respect, the actions of the various social actors are influenced and constrained, but not determined, by the underlying socio-economic structures which pose ideological and pragmatic confinements and dilemmas, thereby occasionally resulting in the emergence of a conflict between espoused ideologies and the needs of the status quo of capitalist economy (Fulcher, 1999). Thus whilst acknowledging that social actors are 'catalysts' for change, Shapiro (1980: 212) points out that educational change 'may proceed only to the extent that is congruent with the needs or goals of that structure'. This being the case, 'it is maintained that "well meaning", individual intentions, constrained by organizational and structural demands, often result in unexpected consequences' (Barton, 1999b: 142).

By implication, it can be held that the attempts at educational reform should not be limited to a focus upon actors' intentions. Rather, the focus should also be placed on the attempts to change the institutional infrastructure of a given socio-political system, along with the processes and norms that are endemic in this infrastructure. An example of the above institutional limitations is manifested in the ways in which inclusion is subordinated to economic ends embodied in the marketization of education and the unfettered quest for effectiveness, standardization and value for money, thereby giving rise to neo-liberal perspectives on inclusion, as discussed in Chapter 1. Within this framework, social actors are trapped in contradictory educational imperatives and demands placed upon them, whereby educators feel pulled in opposite directions by demands to achieve better academic results and promote inclusion (Thomas, 1997; Day, 2005; Sindelar et al., 2006).

Summary

Given the complexity of issues, there is no rational model in legislation, as written policy is not always translated into enacted policy, thus leading to failure in enforcing national or government policy. The failure of government policy cannot be merely explained based on the 'gap' model of educational policy. This would be a rather simplistic and reductionist explanation, in the sense that it depoliticizes educational practices and assigns power only to government or politicians (Fulcher, 1999). In other words, the limitation of policymaking to the examination of policy 'formulation' and 'implementation' as distinct processes is a dichotomous process that fails to give prominence to the dynamic and reciprocal relationship of these instances of policymaking, resulting from the interplay of macro and micro political processes. Raab (1994: 14) points out that the monodimensional models of sequential policymaking presuppose an 'imperative command through hierarchies that overlook the powerful interactive force of networks and/or other structures and actors in a world of pluralistic policy-making' (cited in Berkout and Wielemans, 1999: 404). In consequence, the distinction between 'formulation' and 'implementation' is substituted by the conception of policy processes as generated and implemented 'within and around the educational system' (Ball and Bowe, 1992: 98).

Reflective Exercise

How do you understand the metaphor of educational policymaking as a struggle?

How do you understand the complex, contradictory and contested character of inclusive education policymaking?

Useful Websites

International Bureau of Education – Policy Briefs

    www.ibe.unesco.org/en/themes/curricular-themes/inclusive-education/policy-briefs.html

Enabling Education Network

    www.eenet.org.uk/

The Department for Education

    www.education.gov.uk/

5

Defining the Notion of Ideology: The Interplay of Ideas

Introduction

In this chapter the aim will be to selectively explain some of the definitions of ideology and elucidate the most prominent parameters and processes implicated therein. Simultaneously, it will be possible to explicate the ways in which ideology is interlinked both with actors and structures in a reciprocal and complex relationship. Having done this, it will be possible to begin to provide a conceptual framework with regard to the ways in which a pluralistic model of inclusive education policy analysis can be formulated and implemented.

Educational policy is embedded within a plethora of complementary and adversarial parameters that intersect and produce a 'complex chain effect' (Welton and Evans, 1986: 213; cited in Fulcher, 1990: 3) or in other words, a multidimensional and interactive network, which comprises both structures and actors. This perspective is predicated upon an all encompassing frame-work, contingent on interdependencies and interactions, and which provides a more holistic outlook of educational policymaking (Squipp, 1984), with the emphasis placed upon the 'dual interplay of agency and structure in the crea-tion of historical periods' (Ranson, 1995: 442).This holistic outlook is a fun-damental element and indispensable prerequisite of critical policy analysis whereby the aim is to disassemble the contextual backdrop of educational policymaking through the:

> examination of the politics and ideologies and interest groups of the policy making process; the making visible of internal contradictions within policy formulations, and the wider structuring and constraining effects of the social and economic relations within which policy making is taking place. (Grace, 1991: 26)

Given this interconnective framework, the role that ideology plays in the for-mation of policy is crucial, as ideology is variously interlinked with power, politics and socio-economic structures. As Ball contends (1990: 5): 'A finer, more precise identification of ideologies and influences is necessary to cap-ture the complexity of recent educational policymaking'.

The notion of ideology, and its various linguistic configurations and conceptual affinities (e.g., values and beliefs), feature prominently in many accounts and debates around inclusive education policymaking. Hence, the notion needs to be unpacked in order to understand the ways in which it is linked to, and affects, the processes and outcomes of educational policy-making. The theory of ideology can potentially offer alternative theoretical and conceptual credentials in order to deconstruct and destabilize unequal power relations, value-laden assumptions and vested interests, which give rise to individual deficit accounts and binary perspectives on 'normality' and 'abnormality'. The notion of abnormality is embodied in the emergence and proliferation of categories of 'disability' and 'need' based on a number of perceived deviations from normative ontological assumptions. Sociological analyses of disability and special educational needs highlight the centrality of ideology and point to the necessity to explore the

> relationship(s) between specific types of categories [of disability] and the dominant ideologies of the wider social order . . . An adequate analysis of the generation of these categories, the purposes they serve and the assumptions they involve, must include a consideration of the interplay of historical, political and institutional forces. (Barton, 1986: 274)

The following analysis is not only concerned with providing a definition of ideology within the context of inclusive educational policymaking, but is also concerned with forging theoretical links with the notions of language, discourse and educational policymaking, the aim being to provide a comprehensive conceptual framework of interactive relations and consequential policy effects impacting the processes and outcomes of inclusive education policymaking.

Understanding ideology

The notion of ideology, the delimitation of which in a single definition would seem utterly inappropriate, can be seen from a multitude of perspectives and angles. Eagleton (1991) refers to more than 15 definitions of the word, whilst Dale (1986) suggests that ideology is a 'conceptual chameleon' (cited in Burbules, 1992), thus implying its multidimensional character. Not surprising then, it can be held that the emergence of the various definitions of ideology render the word in a way insignificant since, according to Eagleton (1991: 7), 'any word which covers everything . . . dwindles to an empty sound'. However, notwithstanding these scepticisms, ideology is 'at work in everything we experience as reality' (Zizek, 1994: 17) and it is, therefore, essential, that it is selectively defined and analyzed according to the intended scope of analysis.

Ideology can be characterized as an overarching word that encompasses three levels of knowledge or conceptions of knowledge that are interlinked and interactive. The three levels of knowledge consist of the world that is 'out there' as a separate and objective entity (reality), the world as perceived and interpreted by the characteristics of the human mind (thought), and the way that this understanding (or thought) is reshaped by the unique characteristics of a particular society (Watt, 1994). Thus, ideology encompasses both cognitive and affective elements whereby the latter outweigh the former. It can be held as Eagleton (1991: 19) comments, that ideology 'typically displays a certain ratio between empirical propositions and what we might roughly term a "world view", in which the latter has an edge over the former'. Ideology, however, is defined not only as the accumulative result of values and belief systems, but also as a matter of power. The definitions of ideology can, therefore, be placed on a continuum, the two edges of which offer different standpoints.

The first version of ideology, which is concerned with values and beliefs, is the 'universal version' of ideology (Watt, 1994) or the 'neutral conception of ideology' (Thompson, 1984). Within this version, ideology is defined as the accumulative result of various 'conceptual schemes' that select the most important features from the world and construe new meanings about reality (Watt, 1994). From this perspective, the debate whether ideology is premised upon truth or falsehood is, as Althusser (cited in Eagleton, 1991) purports, in a way groundless because ideology is actually the way through which someone 'lives' her relations to society and, therefore, it cannot be based on erroneous grounds. Thus the conceptual schemes that construe ideology are in essence a selective conceptualization of the allegedly most important elements of the world rather than 'a distorted or fabricated' representation of it (Watt, 1994: 218). In the same vein, Thompson (1984: 6) writes that ideology 'is not a pale image of the social but it is a part of that world. . .' Thus the role of ideology, as a poststructuralist form of social analysis, which questions the existence of an external and objective social world, becomes important and needs critical examination and consideration.

From this perspective, Mannheim disavows the existence of objective truth, in spite of the fact that some people might construe more accurate representations of it. Similarly, Berger and Luckmann (1971) advocate relativism and the 'social construction of reality' (embodied in the notion of constructivism) (cited in Watt, 1994). Anderson (1990: 43) refers to the 'critical' or 'radical' constructivist view according to which, 'the structures of knowledge within society are generated through social interaction and are closely related, if they are not derived from, interests of different groups within the social structure. . . .'

This is consistent with the postmodernist view of relativism, which eschews fixed and preordained notions of reality and knowledge, and thereby aims at challenging and 'deconstructing' these certainties. Likewise, Foucault talks about the existence of multiple 'knowledges' that are constructed by different people implicated within different power relations. In this respect, '"Truth" is linked in a circular relation with systems of power which produce and sustain it, and to effects of power which it induces and which extend it. A regime of truth' (Foucault, 1980a: 133). Particularly, ideology for Foucault is not gauged against the binary poles of truth or false statements, and that is why he eventually dropped the use of ideology for the term 'discourse'. Thus, the crucial distinction regarding the notion of ideology does not lie in the arbitration of the extent to which an ideology is true or false, but rather is concerned with providing the theoretical and methodological credentials for seeing 'historically how effects of truth are produced within discourses, which in themselves are neither true or false' (Foucault, 1980c: 118).

Understandably, the second definition of ideology is implicated with power and is concerned with the emergence of truth and knowledge through relations of domination. This is the critical conception of ideology whereby ideology is given negative connotations and is encapsulated as a process of 'sustaining asymmetrical relations of power that is a process of maintaining domination' (Thompson, 1984: 4). From this perspective, 'ideology' is deployed by the ruling class and used as a means to dominate and exert influence on other peoples' thinking. 'The ideas of the ruling class are in every epoch the ruling ideas: i.e., the class which is the ruling material force in a society is at the same time the ruling intellectual force' (Marx and Engels, 1932/1976: 67; cited in Watt, 1994: 2). Domination, should not, however, as Thompson (1984: 130) asserts, be perceived merely as a relation between the classes. Relations of domination are inherent in 'between nation states, between ethnic groups and between the sexes. . . .' Hence, relations of domination are everywhere and in every aspect of social life, whereby special education does not constitute an exception.

Wherever ideology is perceived and analyzed as a question of power, it raises important issues concerning its credibility with regard to the selective interpretation of the world as it is believed to present an 'inverted picture of reality' predicated on non-scientific grounds (Marx and Engels, 1947: 47; cited in Burbules, 1992: 9) with the ulterior motive to '"mystify" the situation, circumstance or experience of subordinate classes or dominated groups' (Purvis and Hunt, 1993: 478). In so doing, it is more difficult to interrogate the ideological status quo and expunge the subordinating and corrosive effects of ideology. The mystified and intricately complicated attributes of ideologies are proliferated by the fact that ideologies are never 'single'. Therefore the process of disentanglement should be directed according to Blommaert (2005: 175) at 'complexes of Ideological elements often seemingly incongruous with one another, but brought in action – "articulated" or "entextualised" as a single ideology'.

Thus, notwithstanding the notion that ideology is primarily a matter of 'lived relations', some values and beliefs, which are entrenched within theses lived relations may be subjected to criticisms of truth or falsehood. Thus Skillen, an advocator of this case, raises the following pertinent questions; 'Sexist ideologies do not (distortingly) represent women as naturally inferior? Racist ideologies do not confine non-whites to perpetual savagery?'

(cited in Eagleton, 1991). From this perspective, reality is not only selectively interpreted and constructed, but is also misinterpreted and distorted. In consequence, certain claims and beliefs, that are either false or arbitrary, are erroneously and purposefully presented by certain groups as fair and logical. Social structures and institutions bolster the misinterpretations of those powerful and suppressive groups, and impede less privileged people to foreground their own interpretations to the 'collective understanding of the world' (Watt, 1994: 214).

In terms of disability, the 'ideology of control', firmly rooted in arbitrary fabrications of normality, has historically placed the attention upon disabled individual's needs rather than rights, and legitimized the corrosive processes of unequal power relations that instigated all kinds of paternalistic behaviour in the education system. The focus has been on the presumed needs and deficiencies of these students and the necessity to introduce remedial strategies and compensatory measures of support.

Fitch (2003) explores the role of ideology in constructing disabled students' ability, status and social identity. Students' identities are regarded as being ideologically mediated constructs that are constantly negotiated and transformed. Hence, disabled students' 'subordinated' and 'deficient' identities are very thinly related to their attributes that can clearly and unequivocally be identified and categorized and are much more contingent on dominant ideological constructs. As Fitch (2003: 247) writes:

> Subject positions are considered to be actively constructed in conversations and available story lines (Davies and Harre, 2000). But, certain 'conversations' and 'story lines' have ideological and political significance far beyond others. The ideological hegemony of traditionalist/biomedical discourse in special education is a prime example. . . . Therefore, the meaning of a statement such as 'Brenda is a special education student' is saturated with a particular historical and ideological significance. Thus, Brenda's identity can be seen as ideologically constructed at a particular moment in the conversation.

Special education professionals have been historically institutionally empowered to exert an 'ideological control' over disabled students. The professionalization (Fulcher, 1999: 27) of disability assigns power to professionals whose judgements perform an ideological function and place them as gatekeepers to the various forms of institutionalized care (Barton and Tomlinson, 1981). Professionalization is embedded in the psychological discourse, where testing is primarily aimed to determine the institutional placement of the individual.

Professionals have been a powerful means for excluding disabled people, exerting in that way what Kenworthy and Wittaker (2000: 220) call 'professional abuse', as they have been statutorily and institutionally empowered to impose their 'will to truth' (Foucault, 1984a: 114) through the ritualized processes of identification and assessment. Scientific expertise legitimizes professionals' hegemonic role and perpetuates relations of domination over disabled people and their advocates. As Morton and Gipson (2003: 10) so pertinently write: 'This makes the professional the expert, with great authority to pronounce upon the individual, the client. These roles are seen as the natural state of affairs'.

The empowerment of these professionals poses not only political but also moral questions since their 'clients', as Tomlinson and Barton (1981: 17) write, are 'at the receiving end of a decision-making process'. Thus, quoting Wedell (1998) the moral question is 'Who's been God, in making decisions for these kids? What is most important for them in the future?' (in Clough and Corbett 2000: 12). Student's placement in mainstream schools, far from being regarded as a matter of entitlement, has been contingent on the unfettered decision-making 'regimes' of professionals that have been instigated, inter alia, by vested interests and economic concerns (Tomlinson, 1982; Barnes and Mercer, 2005). Rieser (2000: 110), a disabled person himself, is explicit when saying: 'Other people's (usually non-disabled professionals') assessments of us are used to determine where we go to school; what support we get; what type of education; where we live . . .'

Ideology, in this respect, can be characterized as a means of control disseminated within all arenas of a socio-political system. It is used by certain groups to legitimate their domination and impose their 'own understanding of the world' on the less privileged groups, thus endorsing their *hegemony* [their dominant position] (Gramsci, 1971; cited in Drake, 1999). As Leonardo (2003: 209) eloquently writes: '*Even making sense of the world is necessarily implicated with issues of power and, therefore, is a process implicated in relations of domination*' [emphasis in the original]. The 'arbitrarily constructed reality', therefore, is constricted to certain groups who hold political and administrative power that enables them to have their reality 'accepted as true by those whose interests may not necessarily be served by accepting it' (Fiske, 1989: 150; cited in Apple, 2000a: 143).

For Marx and Engels, the theory of ideology has the potential to expose inconspicuous impositions of power and ultimately deconstruct unequal power relations. Ideology, in this respect, is placed in a wider framework and regarded, theoretically, as a potent means of political and social change. As Marx (1975b: 423) suggested: 'the philosophers have only *interpreted* the world in various ways; the point is to *change* it' (cited in Billing, 1991: 4) [emphasis in original]. Accordingly, Burbules (1992: 11) talks about the notion of ideology-critique, where the focus is placed upon deconstruction, which aims to expose the arbitrary constitution of truth, meaning and values, and to divulge the mechanisms which construe these illusionary 'realities'. In terms of special and inclusive education, the focus should be on deconstructing normative assumptions of normality (Graham and Slee, 2008b) and educational practices that render current schooling 'a site in which bodies are compared, differentiated, hierarchized, diagnosed; in which judgements of normality and abnormality are made' (Sullivan, 2005: 29).

In line with the above considerations, it is useful to refer to another dimension of ideology which overlaps both previously referred definitions of ideology and can be viewed from a different perspective. Some 'conceptual schemes' can be perceived in pejorative terms and characterized as 'ideological'. Given the above considerations, debate concerning the viability of inclusive education policies finds many anti-inclusionist theorists committing themselves to 'pragmatism'. By implication, they denounce the notions that advocate towards inclusion and assign them to the 'sphere' of ideology. In particular, Brantlinger (1997), while quoting pertinent examples, criticizes those who adhere to the legacy of special education. In order to defend their negative stance against inclusion, they characterize inclusionists' ideas as 'ideological'. What they fail to do, however, is to identify ideology in their own work. This indicates, as Brantlinger (1997: 436) poignantly puts it, that:

> they are naïve, perhaps because they have 'not read widely cross nationally or cross-disciplines' (Delamont and Atkinson, 1995: 3) and hence remain uniformed by important, relevant work in other fields. Because they refer to others' ideology so pejoratively, their ignorance cannot be excused as benign.

Language, ideology, power relations and educational policymaking

This section concentrates on examining the ways in which power is disseminated, implicated and materialized within the 'social construction of reality' and has an impact on the policymaking process. Given this interconnected framework, the role that ideology plays in the formation of policy is crucial, as ideology is variously interlinked with power, politics and socio-economic structures. Central to analyzing ideology in terms of power relations is language because an 'ideology, like a culture, is carried through language' (Ballard, 2005: 97).

The centrality of language is especially true when we want to analyze ideology in terms of power relations. As Bourdieu (1977) pertinently puts it, 'Language is not only an instrument of communication or even knowledge but also an instrument of power'. 'One seeks not only to be understood but also to be believed, obeyed, respected, distinguished' (cited in Thompson, 1984: 131). Having said this, the role of language and its pervasive effects on constituting subject positions and exclusionary educational practices need to be thoroughly explored and discussed.

Corker (1999: 208) provides an insightful analysis of the necessity to develop the discursive dimension of disability theory through *reflexive knowledge* that 'opens up political discourse to issues of language and difference and their relationship to the unequal distribution of social resources'. In this respect, the critical analysis of language in conjunction with other post-functional strands of disability theory, offers 'a greater range of positions from which disabled people can subvert hegemony and act in the social and political arenas' (Corker, 1999: 209) (see Chapter 3).

It needs noting however, that it is oversimplified and questionable to assert that language always constitutes an instrument of power. Despite the fact that Nietzsche's and Foucault's assertion that power exists everywhere is indubitable, it is important as Eagleton (1991: 9) suggests to distinguish between more and less significant instances of it. By the same token, it is important to distinguish those instances whereby language really matters as it constitutes 'an essential element of the social' (Purvis and Hunt, 1993: 480). Language, in this respect, should not be regarded in isolation from its social context and, in consequence, ideology, which is constituted by language, should be better considered as 'as a matter of discourse than language' (ibid) whereby the former is defined as being the result of language-use, which constitutes a coherent ensemble of ideas/regimes that exert social control by rendering some things 'common sense' (Youdell, 2006: 36). As Baxter (2003: 46) writes:

> . . . discourses are forms of 'knowledge' – powerful sets of assumptions, expectations, and explanations – governing mainstream social and cultural practices. They are systematic ways of making sense of the world by determining power relations within all texts, including spoken interaction.

The importance of language, therefore, as a means of power is materialized through the notion of 'discourse', which 'refers not only to the meaning of language but also to the real effects of language-use, to the material-ity of language' (Codd, 1988: 242). As Fairclough (2000: 1) contends while analyzing the opaque ways in which language is used to veil relations of domination: 'Looked at from a language perspective, different representa-tions/visions of the world are different "discourses"'. In other words, the essence and therefore the power of language is manifested within a partic-ular socio-political context and, in particular, within the discursive proc-esses of this context, which produce and sustain relations of power. These relations of power are constantly constituted and regenerated within the institutional conditions of a particular socio-political system, which pro-duce, sustain and ultimately legitimate asymmetrical relations of power. Throughout the policymaking process (both in terms of policy formula-tion and enactment):

> Language is deployed in the attempt to produce certain meanings and effects . . . discourses also produce social positions 'from which people are "invited" (sum-moned to speak, listen, act, read, work, think, feel, behave and value' (Gee et al., 1996: 10) . . . Policies are very specific and practical regimes of truth and value, and the ways in which policies are spoken and spoken about, their vocabularies, are part of the creation of their conditions of acceptance and enactment. They construct the inevitable and the necessary. (Ball, 2009: 5)

Language is thus understood as being a pervasive means of power that is mate-rialized through discourse and permeates both actors and structures. Fulcher (1999) stresses the fact that language is used as a weapon to exclude, albeit that it has recently veered towards a more 'inclusive' lexicon. It is occasion-ally the case that concerns for parity and human rights are undermined by the 'political elasticity of language' reflected in the 'clauses of conditionality' (Slee, 1996a: 107) that surface strongly within inclusive educational policies. This said, in spite of the fact that the principles of equity and human rights are enthusiastically promulgated, inclusive education policy documents are occasionally riddled with antithetical discourses where:

> Different vocabularies which espouse rights and equity are now used to describe the cosmetic adjustments to traditional practices, which when applied, maintain the powerlessness of disabled students . . . and privileges of those professionals who work 'in their best interests'. (Slee, 1996a: 107)

Fulcher (1999: 3) discusses the crucial role that discourses play in defining the ways in which policy is interpreted and acted upon. In particular, while reflecting on certain local practices, she writes: 'I saw that how language is used matters. It was the instrument of power'. Similarly, Corbett (1996: 32) writes about the deconstruction of language in special education and contemplates that 'Language reflects conceptions of reality or truth'. These relations of power are constantly constituted and regenerated within institutional conditions, which produce, sustain and ultimately legitimate the asymmetrical relations of power. Similarly, Ball (2009: 5) talks about the language of policy and the ways in which it is linked to 'policy rhetoric and discourses'. The emphasis is not on language per se but on the ways in which

> . . . policy discourses work to privilege certain ideas and topics and speakers and exclude others. Policy discourses also organize their own specific rationalities, making particular sets of ideas obvious, common sense and 'true'. Discourses mobilize truth claims and constitute rather than simply reflect social reality. (Ball, 2009: 5)

The power that emanates from the various discourses is thus implicated within institutional conditions and the social structure through which power materializes and affects policy formulation and implementation. This power is differently defined by Billing (1991: 4) as the 'ruling rhetoric', whereby the pervasiveness of language is manifested through, according to Marx and Engels, the social functions of ideas. Quoting Ball (1990: 8),

> Meaning thus arises not from language but from institutional practices, from power relations . . . Words and concepts change their meaning and their effects as they are deployed within different discourses.

Foucault is especially concerned with the discreet imposition of power. Notwithstanding the progress that the various institutions (e.g., schools, prisons, hospitals) have allegedly made during the twentieth century, Foucault is concerned with the ways in which surveillance is inconspicuously underpinning the discursive practices of these institutions (Foucault, 1977a), whereby the notion of 'governemntality' becomes integral to the inconspicuous impositions of self governance (Dean, 2010). As Codd (1988: 243) writes about the nature of power:

> The power that is exercised through discourse is a form of power which permeates the deepest recesses of civil society and provides the material conditions in

which individuals are produced both as subjects and as objects. It is this form of power which is exercised through the discourses of the law, of medicine, psychology and education.

In particular, as far as inclusive education policy is concerned, the representation and maintenance of deficit-oriented discourses create a plethora of powerful ideological and conceptual confinements that 'penetrate consciousness'(Codd, 1988: 242) and are gradually materialized and reconfigured as self governance regimes (Foucault, 1979a). Eventually, wrong discourses assign flawed meanings to the ways in which inclusion is perceived and enacted, as they are sustained by the institutional conditions of a given socio-political system. Notwithstanding the fact that the widespread isolation and institutionalization of disabled students have been challenged to a considerable extent, discriminatory practices are still evasively present, while segregation is still ordered in inconspicuous, yet powerful ways. Inevitably then, 'What has transpired is, as Bernstein (1996) demonstrates, better described as the submersion of special education interest within the discursive noises (Ball, 1988) of integration and latterly inclusion' (Slee, 1997: 407).

Slee and Allan (2001) talk about the role of 'deconstruction', a form of research in inclusive educational policy making, concerned with a 'deconstructive' reading intended to question and destabilize current policies and practices that are erroneously presented as being inclusive. Deconstructive reading or 'dismantling' and 'disassembling critique' (Peters, 1999, para. 6.1) are concerned with exposing the power/knowledge grid that constitutes inclusive education policymaking. Based on the assumption expressed by the philosopher-comic Anthony Hancock that 'Underneath the hand-made crocodile shoes there are still toes' (in Slee and Allan, 2001: 174), deconstructive reading aims to unveil the resilience of traditional forms of special education within an inclusive educational policy discourse, providing evidence of the illusion of progress, albeit ample rhetoric around inclusion. As Slee and Allan (2001: 180) put it: 'We suggest that deconstruction can help us to read policy documents around their own "blind spot" (Patric, 1996: 139) and to disrupt their own "decidability"' (p.141). Similarly, Danziger (1995: 439) gives prominence to the importance of deconstructing the linguistic obscurity of the ostensibly innocuous linguistic constructs underpinning inclusive education policy and practice. As she puts it: 'The danger is that the invisibility of language – its capacity to conceal presuppositions and even political intentions not only from the listener but from the speaker as well – can have unexpected and dire consequences.'

Even single words embody and disseminate the pervasive effects of discourse for they are bearers of ideological presuppositions and preferential standpoints that are conveyed, proliferated and materialized through discursive processes and practices. Thus discourses are not only instantiated in texts (Janks, 1997) but also in single words whereby 'the uses and abuses of language frame meanings that disable and exclude' (Slee, 2001b: 168). Centring upon the linguistic utterances should be an indispensable component of policy analysis:

> . . . the language of policy is important. Part of the work of policy is done in and through policy texts, written and spoken, and the ways in which these represent policy subjects – teachers, learners . . . Policies to greater or lesser extent have a semantic and ontological force. They play their part in the construction of a social world of meanings, of causes and effects, of relationships, of imperatives and inevitabilities. (Ball, 2009:13)

For instance, Runswick-Cole and Hodge (2009: 198) discuss the subjectifying role of the language of 'special educational needs' that ascribes to and consolidates a deficit oriented perspective with regard to the ways in which certain groups of children are positioned in education:

> Indeed, the language of 'special educational needs' within current policy and legislation continues to locate the 'problem' within the child . . . In the education system, language is able to create positive and negative images of children which, in turn, impact on the policy and practice of education . . . Indeed, an overview of the development of the use of language in special education policy demonstrates the power of language over the lives of children.

Hence, the process towards the realization of an inclusive discourse necessitates a conscious and explicit attempt to deconstruct the ways in which language is used to frame meanings and ascribe social identities. As Luke (1995: 41) contends, 'It is extremely risky to engage in the construction of texts of curriculum, education policy and research without some explicit reflexivity on how and whom we construct and position in our talk and writing'.

Critical Discourse Analysis (CDA) can be utilized as a liberating theoretical and analytical tool in highlighting and unveiling the ways in which language is a powerful mechanism of social control. CDA constitutes an attempt to go beyond conventional methods of analysis, as it opens up new theoretical avenues in order to unveil unequal power relationships embodied in language. It can delve into the subtle linguistic characteristics of texts and speech with a view to identifying the power relationships embedded in them and unveiling relationships of domination (Kress, 1990; Fairclough, 2001). As Mills (1997: 134) writes, CDA is concerned 'with questions of possible meanings of different discourses used by participants in speech and in text', along with the ways in which these meanings are inexorably linked to power.

CDA also aims to expose the subjectifying effects of certain discourses and explore their 'constructive effects . . . upon social identities, social relations and systems of knowledge and belief' (Fairclough, 1992: 12), thereby destabilizing the ways in which these constructive effects become a legitimized and naturalized way of accepting and legitimizing inequality (Van Dijk, 2001). In so doing it is possible to identify and make transparent the opaque ways in which unequal power relations lead to the disempowerment of disabled people (Liasidou, 2008a, 2011) with a view to mobilizing progressive social change (Kress, 1990; Fairclough, 2001). As Fairclough (1999: 97) writes:

> [CDA] . . . sets out to make visible through analysis, and to criticize, connections between properties of texts and social processes and relations (ideologies, power relations) which are generally not obvious to people who produce and interpret those texts, and whose effectiveness depends upon this opacity.

This discursive analytic approach concentrates on the structure (linguistic description) of the text, as well as the interactive processes of the text linked to the stages of interpretation and explanation, the latter stages offering an interdiscursive analytical insight into the micro/macro structures underpinning power relationships. Fairclough (2001: 91) articulates ten questions concerned with the vocabulary, the grammar and the textual structures of the text, against which the descriptive analysis of the text should take place.

Simultaneously, in attempting to expose and explicate the importance of language and its ideological effects, the focus should also be on the 'discursive absences' (Stenson and Watt, 1999; Fairclough, 2000) of the text that have an equally pervasive impact on the ways that disabled children are positioned and constructed within legislative documents. The 'linguistic silences' or 'absences' of texts are also embodiments of the pervasive effect of discourses implicated in the policymaking agenda. Luke (2002: 104) draws upon Derrida's (1980) analyses of absence and silence in order to denote the fact that the '"unsaid" and the "unwritten", can be as significant as what is said'. As Slee (2001c: 114) contends, 'in the absence of a stipulative language of inclusive education, inclusive schooling represents a default vocabulary for 'assimilation' and thereby exclusion. Understandably, the 'silences' of the official discourse and its inability to conjure up the necessity to reverse unequal power relations endemic to mainstream schooling bring to bear profound implications for the ways in which inclusive education policy is conceptualized and implemented. The individualistic and pathologizing gaze obscures the 'needs' and, thereby, deficiencies of the educational system as nothing is said about the necessity to reconsider the nature of schooling, the curriculum and the teaching styles, as well as the exclusionary policies and practices firmly embedded in processes and practices of current schooling .

In effect, what has come to be termed as 'discourse analysis' should also encompass the analysis of the institutional and structural elements of the social world (Thompson, 1984) along with the ways in which subjectivities are 'interpellated' (Althusser, 1994) and, hence, constituted and positioned through the prevalent ideological constructs. The essence of discourse, therefore, and the asymmetrical power relations that saturate such a discourse, encompasses a multi-angled perspective. In this sense,

> . . . the notion of discourse has to be stretched to include the messages embedded in curricula, pedagogy and the organization of pupils for learning, as well as those generated through spatialising discourses of urban planning, the design and purpose of buildings and the sorting, labelling and placing of people. (Armstrong, 2002: 55)

The emphasis of policy documents as text should, therefore, extend to include the context or the 'broad discursive field within which policies are developed and implemented' (Taylor, 1997: 25), with the aim not only to better conceptualize policy, but also to demonstrate or deconstruct the subtle interactions between the various processes implicated therein, and expose any invisible and unobtrusive, albeit corrosive, forms of power. The pervasiveness of discourse is manifested within the processes 'whereby interests of a certain kind become masked, rationalised, legitimated in the name of certain forms of political power . . .' (Eagleton, 1991: 202).

The failure of inclusive educational policies might be attributed to the 'deeply entrenched discourse of disability and of the institutionalised bases which construct that discourse' (Fulcher, 1990: 16). For instance, the process of ab-normalization has exerted a prodigious ideological effect on shaping dominant thinking with regard to the notion of 'difference' on the basis of ability. Campbell (2005: 113) explores the subjectifying role of legislation that assigns people to fixed ontological categories (e.g., disability). These people are portrayed as being negatively different and 'disability is assumed to be onto-logically intolerable, that is, *inherently* negative' (ibid.: 109). These assumptions underpin, according to Campbell (2005: 109), 'most of the claims of disability discrimination that are juridically sanctioned within the welfare state and is imbricated in compensatory initiatives and the compulsion towards therapeutic interventions'.

Reflective Exercise

In what ways can language become a powerful means for exerting social control?

Why is it important to have an informed awareness of how and what we construct through language?

Ideology and the interplay of action and structure: an exploratory agenda

Given that educational policies are in a dynamic and reciprocal relation with the wider socio-political contexts, it is important to offer a multilevel histori-cal and sociological account of the conceptualization of educational policy, along with some interpretations of the parameters that shape inclusive educa-tion policy and have an impact on the translation of policy into practice. This convergent conceptual framework has the potential to delineate the multiple and reciprocal relations between values and materials, which beget policy 'contextualization' and 'recontextualization' (Ball, 1994b).

Ball (1994b) exemplifies the difference between 'policy as discourse' and 'policy as text'. On the one hand, the 'policy as discourse' metaphor gives prominence to the 'public face' of policy and the ways in which official policies set out the 'discursive contours' (Liasidou, 2008a) within which policy imple-mentation takes place. The 'policy as text' metaphor highlights the mediated role of social actors, who interpret official policy in varied ways depending on their own understandings, perspectives and vested interests and, hence, considers them as being important policymakers within their contexts of practice (Croll and Moses, 1989) for they can either facilitate or impede trans-formative change through their 'enacted policies' (Ball and Bowe, 1992). From this perspective, as already discussed in Chapter 4, educational practitioners acquire a pre-eminent position in the policymaking process, as policy interpretation and, hence, implementation rests on their discretionary power to interpret and recontextualize policy according to their own understandings, values and predispositions. The contradictions and dilemmas inherent in the policy agendas are infiltrated through educational practitioners' understandings and ideologies, thereby confounding their role to deal effectively with the 'intellectual, social and emotional complexities of schools in challenging circumstances . . .' (Day 2005: 575).

Hence, transformative changes rest upon a complex and reciprocally related web of macro and micro dynamics. Changes are instigated by an interactive framework of ideological, and structural dynamics, which jointly collude towards the transformation of the current state of affairs. These forces and the power relations immanent in them that act upon bringing educational change are located both within actors and structures. Social actors alone cannot, thus, bring change unless the institutional infrastructure (e.g., legislation) of a socio-political system is favourably positioned towards these changes. Change is instigated by an array of elements that are congruent to the emergence of the dominant 'particular forms of reasoning and "telling the truth" . . . and kinds of knowledge central to establishing a particular discourse . . .' (Popkerwitz and Brennan, 1998: 15).

The debate around the interplay of agency and structures, and their role in the process of change, is a refractory one that has long bedevilled both theorists and theoretical movements in general. First of all, it is important to examine the positions which lean either towards an overemphasis of the action-oriented position or towards the structural one. The ultimate aim is to overcome dichotomous thinking in relation to the two positions and offer a more balanced and dialectical account, viable enough to provide a comprehensive analysis of the ways that ideology is interlinked with structural institutions within the interplay of power and domination.

Marxist accounts give prominence to the 'infrastructural bases' of ideology, namely to the socio-economic conditions that determine the limits within which the politico-ideological interests are set (Eagleton, 1991: 199). According to Marx (1963: 15), human beings 'make their own history but not in circumstances of their own choosing' (cited in Cohen, 1989: 9). In this respect power is examined in relation to the structural perspectives of the State, while the role of the agent is considered of secondary importance. The notion of the State and of social class is conceptualized 'as objective structures and their relations as an objective system of regular connections, a structure and a system whose agents "men" [sic] are in the words of Marx "bearers of it". . .' (Poulantzas, 1969: 70; cited in Drake, 1999: 20).

This is, however, as discussed earlier (see Chapter 4), a limited and limiting view since it downgrades the role of agent as a potent means of change. It is possible, within the stringent demands imposed by certain institutional conditions, that the 'hazardous play of domination' (Baert, 1998: 125) can be challenged and reversed by certain social actors, thus leading to the subversion of the status quo. In effect, power in Foucault's terms does not always bear negative connotations and, therefore, it is possible to override the pessimistic accounts which downplay the role of agent and negate the productive effects of power. Thus, as Foucault (1988: 123) contends:

> As soon as there is a power relation, there is a possibility of resistance. We can never be ensnared by power: we can always modify its grip in determinate conditions and according to a precise strategy.

By implication, Hindess and Hirst reject the overemphasis on 'infrastructural bases' and stress the importance of political ends and interests, which construct reality. These political ends and interests do not merely derive from social reality, but rather, they constitute the discourses through which social reality emerges (cited in Eagleton, 1991). This position alone, however, is again by itself reductionist as it downplays the role of structural conditions of political action. Thus, in spite of the fact that ideology is 'subject-centred' it is not as Eagleton (1991: 223) writes, 'reducible to the question of subjectivity'. This is because, 'Some of the most powerful ideological effects are generated by institutions . . .' and hence by the structural conditions of a given socio-political context.

What is missing from Marxist and other accounts, therefore, is a conceptualization of ideology in terms of interplay of action and structure. The theory of structuration, articulated by Giddens (1986) and exemplified in the work of Archer (1982), denounces binary considerations and presents an integrated account depicting the interplay between action and institutional and structural conditions. Giddens, for instance, discusses the ways in which social action is intricately interwoven with 'social collectivities' in the production of 'praxis'. That is,

> To speak of praxis as the constitution of social life entails a concern not only for the manner in which conduct, consequences, and relations are generated but also for the conditions which shape and facilitate these processes and outcomes . . . (cited in Cohen, 1989: 12)

Drawing on Giddens' account, Thompson (1984) theorizes the ways in which the three levels of the account are reciprocally related and have varied implications according to the emphasis given. The analytical framework is concerned with the ways in which agents can act within the context of institutional structures, with the possibility of either reproducing these structures or pursuing a transformative action. This is in alignment with a Foucauldian analysis of ideology, whereby individuals can be either deceived, by the ostensibly innocuous nature of ideologies, or be enabled to vehemently break the ideological grip and achieve transformative change, that is congruent, however, with the contextual relations and discourses preceding them (Foucault, 1980c).

Within this conceptual framework, the locus of power can be located within the agents per se, who are able to pursue certain aims and interests, or within the social institutions, which empower the agents to pursue these ends. Had it not been for these institutions, agents would have been unable to pursue them, while in cases where other agents or groups are systematically excluded from this 'institutional empowerment', the situation is characterized as one of domination (Thompson, 1984). For instance, the various professionals that work within the field of special education get empowered by the institutional conditions of bureaucracy, managerialism and proceduralism. Their dominating position is thus rendered 'institutionally sanctioned' (Brantlinger, 1997: 432), and as a result, subverting their domination seems to require the eradication of a whole institutionalized structure, a prospect that, on the face of it, seems an intimidating and, in some respects, a prodigious exercise.

Ball (1990), based on the Althusserian conceptualization of social systems, whereby social structure is conceived of setting limits but not prohibiting meaningful choice in terms of ideological, political and economic levels, tries to disentangle the complexity of educational policy and concomitantly to offer an all-encompassing analytical framework. As Ball (1990: 8) contends, 'One basic task, then, is to plot the changing ideological, economic and political parameters of policy and to relate the ideological, political and economic to the dynamics of policy debate and policy formulation'. In so doing, it is possible to discern, according to Evans (1994), the subtle interrelations of power within the interplay of constraints (structures) and agency, whereby:

> Power is exercised, or practiced, rather than possessed and so circulates through every related force and requires us to examine the way in which power, as a

recursive force and form of practice, is embedded/embodied in every aspect, agent and agency involved in the policy process. (Evans, 1994: 59)

Understandably, inclusive policies cannot be examined in isolation from the profusion of exclusionary practices and the unequal power relations endemic to them. The identification and removal of special education thinking and the deep structures that surround it should be at the core of the struggles for transformative change. Otherwise,

. . . if the deep structures of special education – those issues that underlie relations of power, control, dominance and subordination – are not identified and transformed, exclusion and marginalization will be reproduced even under the most well intentioned and most well supported programmes. (McDonnell, 2003: 267)

Ideologies and the politics of inclusive educational policymaking

In the following analysis the aim will be to examine the ideologies influencing the processes and outcomes of inclusive education policymaking and identify the ways in which the various definitions of ideology are implicated therein. As we have already discussed, policies are not neutral; they reflect underlying ideologies and assumptions in a society, and these ideologies underpin special education policymaking. As Lynd has succinctly observed, 'the controlling factor in any science is the way it views and states its problems' (cited in Boyd, 1992: 505).

It is, therefore, important to present the ideologies upon which the education of disabled students is predicated, the aim being to explicate the ways in which the emergent discursive reality influences the multiple facets of educational policymaking. At first, it is pertinent to examine the predominant ideologies that underlie educational policymaking in general, before proceeding to the examination of ideologies more directly pertaining to inclusive education policymaking in terms of disability and SEN. It needs noting, however, that this distinction is merely made in terms of analytical convenience since all ideologies are reciprocally related in much the same way as the distinction between education and special education becomes blurred and difficult to sustain.

The welfare state and the marketization of education

The ideologies of the market constitute an increasingly dominating imperative within the educational policymaking landscape. These ideologies are referred to as New Right, a strand of which is neo-liberalism, and are characterized by the 'increasing colonization of education policy by economic policy imperatives' (Ball, 1998: 122). Notions like equality and social justice are marginalized (Welch, 1998; Barton and Slee, 1999; Bottery, 2000) and neo-liberal imperatives gain an ascendant role in national educational policymaking agendas (Whitty et al., 1998).

Markets are thus regarded by their advocates as being more democratic than democracy itself (Barton, 1996: 3), as they are believed to be the 'most efficient mode of allocating resources and more responsive to individual needs' (Barton and Slee, 1999: 5). In the United Kingdom, the emergence of New Right ideologies can be traced to the 1970s speech on education by Callaghan, the then UK Prime Minister, at the Ruskin College, Oxford, who discussed issues of assessment of standards, accountability and the relationship between schools and industry (Ball, 2009). Neo-liberal ideologies were thereafter embodied in the educational arrangements initiated by the Educational Reform Act (ERA) in 1988, which marked a significant paradigm shift in the UK educational policy landscape. As Ball (2008: 186) writes:

> The importance of ERA in the history of English Education is undeniable. . . . The education market created by ERA and other legislation gave an impetus to schools to act independently and competitively but at the same time subjected them to the disciplines of market relations as conjured up within Hayekian economic and market theory.

From this perspective, market forces are considered to have the potential to raise standards and efficiency of the education system (Whitty et al., 1998; Bottery, 2000) thereby restoring, as it is claimed, the 'levelling down' of achievement which resulted from the attempts to achieve equal education outcomes for all, and in more general terms, to achieve a just and more equitable society (Whitty, 2002).

Neo-liberalism is thus explicitly against welfare policies and abhors any kind of State intervention in the lives of individuals who are, allegedly, the only ones who know what is the best for them. Inequality between individuals or groups is regarded as a natural feature of modern societies and by no means can social intervention be used as a means to alter the natural state of affairs (Dale and Ozga, 1993). Brantlinger (2004) identifies neo-liberalism as the mega category of 'hierarchical' ideologies that aims to establish social hierarchies through competition and political submission. This is in stark contrast to the 'communal ideology' that recognises human dignity, commonality and equality. Given the prominence of the hierarchical ideology within stratified and economically structured societies, 'working for equity and inclusion is bound to be a struggle' (Bratlinger, 2004: 23).

The focus of neo-liberal ideologies is placed upon competitiveness and on 'commercial rather than educational decision making' (Gewirtz et al., 1993; cited in Barton, 1996: 37) whereby the 'common good is now to be regulated exclusively by the laws of the market, free competition, private ownership and profitability . . .' (Apple 1988: 11; cited in Rizvi and Lingard, 1996: 19). As a result, notions of social justice and collegiality are given a low priority within this framework (Barton and Slee, 1999).

Within such a system as Bottery (2000: 59) contemplates, people are regarded as human resources rather than resourcefully human. Market forces in education, like monopolies in the market place that concentrate power and wealth in the hands of the few, solely promote the rights of the resourceful individuals, who have full access and participation in the wealth of mainstream schools. Given that the market forces in education accentuate competition and provide a monodimensional notion of ability, the rights of the so called 'less able children' 'to take the same risks and seek the same rewards' (Brisenden, 1986: 117; cited in Barton, 1988: 6) are considerably constricted. Ball (2003) talks about the 'Performativity discourse', which is centred upon increased efficiency and effectiveness of the educational apparatus that is solely measured against examination results and subsequent league tables (Ball, 2003). The inevitable emergence of the 'discourse of competition' obliterates the 'lexicon of values' and concomitantly gives rise to the 'lexicon of expediency, pragmatics and financial necessity' (Ball, 1998b: 92).

The ascendancy of neo-liberal imperatives has given rise, according to Ball (2008: 187) to 'local economies of student worth' whereby schools compete in order to recruit 'value adding' students, those most likely to contribute to measurable 'improvements' and 'performance outputs', and those easiest and cheapest to teach, and whose presence attracts others like them. Concomitantly, those students who add 'negative value', those with Special Needs, those for whom English is a second language, or those with social or emotional difficulties are avoided where possible in this economy.

The ascendancy of 'local economies of student worth' within the United Kingdom and across the globe, engender the 'ideal student' (Harwood and Humphy, 2008: 373). The attributes that epitomize the ideal student, are used as a heuristic in order to identify the 'non-ideal students [who] are branded by what was being *done for* them as opposed to what they *can do* or can achieve' (Harwood and Humphy, 2008: 379). As Goodley (2007: 321) writes:

> Too often, when we think of involving students in educational practices, we assume students to be able, productive, skilled, accountable individuals who are ready and willing to lead developments within the classroom. They fit the quintessential construction of the modernist, unitary, humanistic subject (Chinn, 2006). In short, our students are 'able'. Such a construction of the learner is hugely problematic for students with disabilities and or special educational needs who require the support of others. (Goodley, 2007: 321)

'Non-ideal students' are considered as being a counterforce to the ambitious proclamations of rightist ideologies, and are constructed as an unacceptable burden (Ballard, 2004) within fundamentally competitive and meritocratic modern Western societies. As a result, they are relegated to the fringes of mainstream school life and they are regarded as being less than 'docile bodies' (Foucault, 1977a).

An inclusive education reform agenda necessitates re-evaluating the priorities of education systems, and challenging the ways in which they create subordinate and deficient students' identities. Towards this end, it is necessary to mobilize 'cultural' and 'symbolic' changes in current schooling (Artiles et al., 2006: 264), with a view to questioning and deconstructing policies and practices that disempower and devalue certain groups of students.

Reflective Exercise

What conceptions of the 'ideal student' emanate from the predominance of the discourse of marketization?

The ideology of control

Special education has been historically predicated on psychological and medical approaches, which were rooted to the 'predestinative' ideology (Neave, 1977: 13) of individual deficit and legitimated by a humanitarian ideology

(Belanger, 2001). Evidently, this has been a restricting and restricted ideological construct stemming from a 'pathognomonic orientation' (Jordan et al., 1997: 85) of an individual deficit perspective. This kind of 'individualistic gaze' has squarely placed educational failure within the individual attributing it to such factors like 'limited intellectual abilities, linguistic shortcomings, lack of desire and motivation to learn . . .' (Barton and Slee, 1996: 6). Medical discourses assume that disability is about impairment or loss that is 'an observable or intrinsic, objective attribute or characteristic of a person . . .' (Fulcher, 1999: 27). Similarly, some psychological discourses assume that intelligence is innate or inherited and assessment is carried out in order to measure intelligence and assign someone to a certain category.

The eugenic and social Darwinism ideologies, allegedly intended to improve the genetic composition of human species, have given credence, reinforced individual pathology perspectives and consolidated the supremacy of 'nature' and 'heredity' over nurture (Thomas and Loxley, 2007). This paradigm, reiterating Skidmore (1996: 34):

> . . . conceptualises special needs as arising from deficits in the neurological or psychological make-up of the child, analogous to an illness or medical condition. Borrowing from the medical discipline, authors often speak of the 'aetiology' of a given syndrome. (cited in Slee, 1998b: 443)

Medical power plays a pervasive role in determining disabled people's educational and life trajectories. Special education procedures and practices pose important ethical issues and considerations as they are inexorably bound up with unequal power relations that construe arbitrary and unidimensional arbitrations of 'ability'. The assessment procedures, the categorization, the delayed admissions (Loxley and Thomas, 1997) and the occasionally subsequent exclusion of disabled students are dependent upon the 'unfettered discretion' of professionals (Fulcher, 1999: 116), which promotes their hegemonic ascendancy and simultaneously disempowers disabled children and their parents, whose voices are subordinated. Some commentators go so far as to suggest that the 'assessment procedures are barely more accurate than a flip of the coin' (Christensen, 1996: 66).

This is particularly true for non-normative categories of disability (Tomlinson, 1982), which are not clear-cut and depend more on the values, beliefs and interests of people making the judgments, than on any characteristics intrinsic to the students. These are, for instance, students designated as having learning difficulties, social, emotional and behavioural difficulties, attention deficit disorders. Graham and Jahnukainen (2011) refer to the increase of identification rates in non-normative categories of disability. This is in stark contrast to the decrease of identification rates in traditional normative categories of disability like sensory, physical and severe intellectual impairment. The proliferation of identification rates in non-normative categories is a testament to the host of social and cultural dynamics, as well as individual and professional interests that are implicated in the identification and categorization processes of special education.

The notion of disability is placed against an arbitrarily constructed notion of normality, and, by implication, the 'normalizing gaze' places special education practice 'into a complex power/knowledge web in which power is exerted over children, whether or not in their (best) interests' (Marshall, 1996: 129). The 'panoptic' technologies of control, as conceptualized and explicated by Foucault (1977a), exercise power through space and, hence, through the spatial shifting of disabled people who are segregated for having transgressed the limits of a socially constructed normality. Once the contours of normality are defined, 'deviants' are put under scrutiny and are subjected to an array of normalizing and segregating processes. Foucault (1977a) emphasized the importance of the 'normalizing judgement' or normalization in the function of normalizing power.

Under these circumstances, practices that are nominated as being 'inclusive' are in essence practices within which a plethora of inconspicuous forms of exclusion are operating (see Chapter 1). These practices restrict inclusion to its spatial dimension by adopting assimilationist perspectives and compensatory measures of support in order to 'normalize' certain individuals through expert intervention and remedy, thereby promoting 'internal' exclusive practices to take place in terms of streaming or grouping of pupils. In that way, Feiler and Gibson (1999: 148) suggest that 'inclusion is jeopardised by a widespread inclination to label and pigeon-hole children' rather than fostering the feeling of inclusivity through structural and pedagogical reorganization of general schooling (Graham and Sweller, 2011).

The redemptive ideologies: The sociological response to disability

The influence of medical and individual deficit perspectives, in conjunction with the dominance of deficit-oriented thinking, delayed sociological analyses in relation to disability. In spite of the fact that issues of social inequality pertaining to ethnicity and gender had already been significantly explored and theorized by sociologists, similar analyses with regard to disability appeared at a later stage (Barton and Oliver, 1992). This belated sociological engagement can be attributed to the overarching influence of biomedical accounts in monopolizing the notion of special educational needs and reducing it to a form of individual inadequacy and pathology. As a result, special education has been traditionally predicated on the assumption that there is a body of unassailable and, hence, rational knowledge that is ahistorical, apolitical and, therefore, value free. Given this, academics and professionals within the field have been hitherto assailed by the thrust to discover and establish, through empirical study, this objective knowledge, and as a corollary to this, eschewed the possibility to 'meddle with the sentimental, the subjective, the sloppy and the politicised' (Thomas and Glenny, 2002: 345), which allegedly distorted the scientific bases of special education.

Delayed sociological interest in the field can also be attributed to the fact that sociologists regarded students educated in special schools as being politically insignificant in contributing to the wider social changes they envisaged (Barton and Oliver, 1992). The profound impact of medical and psychological discourses precipitated negative connotations with regard to disability and portrayed disabled people as pitiful and subordinate creatures. Any perceived physical, emotional and intellectual deviations from conventional notions of normality have been relegated to the sphere of individual pathology. As Barton and Oliver (1992: 68) write:

> . . . special education has been dominated by a form of reductionism which gives a privileged status to individualistic explanations. Within-the-child factors are emphasized encouraging 'special needs' to be viewed as a personal trouble and not a public issue.

That said, even early sociological accounts were solely concerned with functional analyses of disability and SEN and were limited to questions centring upon the number of students identified as having SEN, the nature of their problems and the ways in which these problems could be dealt with and contained (Barton and Tomlinson, 1981).

This kind of analyses have been gradually questioned and substituted by new theoretical and analytical perspectives, with a view to highlighting the intricate interplays of multiple dynamics and unequal power relations impacting on the processes of categorization and selection on the basis of ability. The institutionalization, incarceration and long standing isolation of disabled individuals have been repositioned as unacceptable forms of social oppression that could no longer be unproblematically viewed as the result of humanitarian and progressive practice (Tomlinson, 1982; Barton and Tomlinson, 1984).

Sociological scholarship has recognized the profundity of the issues at hand and provided new epistemological lenses in order to investigate the highly political nature of disability and special educational needs (see also Chapter 3). This approach has sought to critique and 'deconstruct' the hidden assumptions and mechanisms that lie behind disability and special educational needs and document the 'shaky and controversial ground' (Barton and Tomlinson, 1981: 14) upon which special education policy and practice have been based. Absolute arbitrations of ability and 'normalcy' mask the inadequacies of the system to provide for learner diversity. The prevailing rationality of deficit-oriented discourses disregards that many problems cannot be resolved unless certain socio-political factors are acknowledged and challenged, so as to uncover 'the collective responsibility of existing social structures and relations . . .' (Slee, 1996: 110) that engender and perpetuate disabling barriers. Disability is repositioned as being an ideologically, socially and institutionally mediated phenomenon that emanates from and rests upon wider socio-political and cultural contextual factors.

By adopting socio-political frameworks, the discourse of professionalism can be explained in terms of power and 'vested interest'. As Tomlinson (1985: 160) has pointed out 'an understanding of the competition and alliances among interest groups in special education is crucial to understanding its expansion'. The individual-deficit model of disability involves the 'medicalization of the mechanisms of social control' (Barnes et al., 1999: 85) embodied in the role of the various SEN professionals, who have vested interests in preserving and corroborating deficit-oriented perspectives on disability and special educational needs since any change in the 'status quo' is regarded as a threat (Tomlinson, 1982) to their institutionally empowered positions.

The sociological response to disability is analogous to the attempt to provide the 'bigger picture' (Grace, 1991) in educational policymaking, thereby unravelling 'organizational pathology' (Ware, 2002) of current structures and relations. Disability thus goes beyond the individual pathology imperatives, and is placed within an all encompassing agenda. Adopting what C. Wright Mills (1961) calls the 'sociological imagination' the aim is to highlight the relationship between the private and the public and document the ways in which personal issues are interrelated with and rest upon the wider social structure, thereby challenging binary perspectives between biography and history, between 'personal troubles' and 'public issues'. By implication, the assimilationist model of individual pathology is challenged, and through the sociological imagination, disability, as Giddens (1982) suggests, entails a 'critique of existing forms of society' and hence, a critique of existing forms of education, and envisages the awareness of 'alternative futures' (cited in Barnes et al., 1999: 13).

The belated sociological engagement with the political dimension of the notion of 'special educational needs' was subsequently supplemented by sociological analyses concerned with providing a social and political theory of disability (Barton and Oliver, 1992) in order to challenge the dominance of medical and individual models of disability. These models subscribe to a personal tragedy theory of disability, whereby the latter is solely understood as a 'personal problem' subject to medical assessment and diagnosis, through expert and scientific arbitrations of 'deviations' from pre-conceived notions of 'normality'.

The 'politics of silence' characterizing disabled people's invisibility and physical and intellectual incarceration was challenged by disabled people themselves (Union of the Physically Impaired Against Segregation – UPIAS, 1976: section 14). They articulated the necessity to challenge the overarching influence of the medical model of disability over their lives:

> The imposition of medical authority . . . [leading to] the traditional way of dealing with disabled people . . . for doctors and other professionals to decide what is best for us . . .

Drawing on the definition of disability introduced by UPIAS (1976), Oliver inaugurated the social model of disability that drew a discernible line between the impaired self and social structures. Oliver (1990), along with other British sociologists, utilized new epistemological and analytical tools in order to highlight the social, cultural and political dimensions of disability.

The demarcation line drawn between impairment and disability has played a central role in the debates around the complex nature of disability (MacKay, 2002; Thomas, 2001, 2004). The notion of impairment refers to difficulties arising from personal deficits, whereas disability refers to the difficulties arising from society either in terms of its materialist conditions (Oliver, 1990) or in terms of political and cultural dynamics (Shakespeare, 1997; Thomas, 1999).

Disability is no longer linked to individual inadequacy, but rather, is regarded as the result of ideological and structural factors that have been complicit in the emergence of a vast range of disciplinary and normalizing techniques. The 'impaired self' is annihilated by the social model of disability, as the responsibility for its constitution is attributed to disabling social and economic structures. That said, disability is understood as being on par with sexism and racism and it is asserted that 'disability is wholly and exclusively social . . . disablement has nothing to do with the body. It is a consequence of social oppression' (Oliver, 1996: 41–2). As Barnes (1996: 1) writes:

> a growing number of academics, many of whom are disabled people themselves, have re-conceptualised disability as a complex and sophisticated form of social oppression . . . or institutional discrimination on par with sexism, heterosexism and racism . . . theoretical analysis has shifted from individuals and their impairment to disabling environments and social attitudes.

The social model of disability has paved the way for a new political era for disabled people and their advocates as it heralds a new ontology of disability intended to destabilize unidimensional and insular individual pathology accounts prescribed by medicine and psychology. Disability has been reconceptualized and repositioned as a social, political and cultural artefact, arbitrarily construed, reified and sustained in order to safeguard the interests of industrial capitalism (Oliver, 1996). The advent of capitalism in industrialized societies has generated a new ontological category of 'normality', incarnated in 'docile bodies' (Foucault, 1977a) deemed 'fit' and 'capable' enough to contribute to labour market, whereas the 'less than docile bodies' have been increasingly subjected to discriminating and stigmatizing nomenclature and normalizing cultural and institutional procedures, to approximate conventional notions of normality and social order. As Oliver (1999: 3) writes in terms of a materialist analysis of disability:

> The economy, through both the operation of the labour market and the social organisation of work, plays a key role in producing the category disability and in determining societal responses to disabled people.

Despite their pivotal contribution to Disability Studies, Oliver's (1990) theorizations of disability have been widely contested on a number of bases, and instigated a theoretical battle over the validity of the social model of disability to explain fully the complexity of disability. For instance, these initial theorizations have been contested on the basis of their monodimensional materialist analyses of disability, which failed to take into consideration the cultural and ideological bases of disability (Shakespeare, 1997; Thomas, 2004), as well as the ways in which disabled people, and especially women, experience the effects of their impairment (Corker and French, 1999; Thomas, 2001).

Feminist and postmodern/poststructural accounts have been utilized in order to criticize the social model of disability for its perceived failure to explicate fully the experience and complexity of disability (Crow, 1996; Morris, 1996; Shakespeare, 1997; Corker and French, 1999). Feminist analysts, alongside medical sociologists (e.g., Bury, 2000), voiced their concerns over the oversimplification of disability as a social oppression artefact, and expressed their experience of impairment as a factor that contributed to the difficulties they faced. For instance, Morris (1991), a female disabled activist and writer, articulated the necessity to take into consideration the experience of impairment as a factor that contributes to disability.

Understandably, any forms of binary considerations (Peters, 1999) are harmful and create a theoretical impasse that impedes the generation of constructive and liberating theorizations of disability (see Chapter 3). In parallel with racism or sexism, the question is not whether there are differences in gender or colour. Rather the question is whether, and to what extent society marginalizes and oppresses these people on the basis of their differences. Whether we are talking about disability or impairment the crucial issue is to highlight the ways in which society disempowers and subjugates certain groups of people on the basis of their personal attribute, thereby either creating or exacerbating their difficulties. Sociological scholarship moves beyond the questionable and flawed rationality of the defectology discourse and tries to reveal and challenge the societal 'causes' of disability. By doing this, however, it does not attempt to 'mask' disability and conceal its existence. What it attempts to do, is to uncover the societal causes that 'exacerbate' and proliferate disabling and oppressive barriers.

Given the above considerations, Thomas (1999: 125) proposes a 'social relational approach' whereby the personal experience in living with a disability and impairment, along with their interaction, should be at the core of Disability Studies. Similarly, Norwich (2010) foregrounds an 'interactionist causal framework' in dealing with the complexity of special educational needs and disabilities, embodied in what he calls a 'bio-psycho-social model of disability', that is 'a useful way in going beyond the unnecessary polarization between medical (individual) and social models . . .' (Norwich, 2010: 86).

By no means do theoretical contestations undermine the value and validity of the social model of disability that symbolizes the struggles of disabled people 'for equity and a non-oppressive, non-discriminatory world' (Barton, 2003: 11). These theoretical contestations should be seen as 'illustrations of a healthy and exciting dialogue' (Barton, 2003: 10) that permit the cross-fertilization of diverse perspectives and insights. The social model of disability has played a powerful theoretical and political role in inspiring and mobilizing political action for 'a social world in which all people experience the realities of inclusive values and relationships' (Barton, 2003: 11).

Reflective Exercise

How do you understand the social response to disability? What are the implications for education policy and practice?

On what basis has the social model of disability been criticized?

Summary

The previous section has provided the theoretical backdrop against which a political model of policy, based on a theory of discourse, has been presented and explicated. Educational policy is conceptualized and shaped within the interplay of unequal power relations, whereby the different loci of power act in every arena of a socio-political system both synchronically and diachronically. If we are genuinely interested in understanding the complex nature of inclusive education policies we should seek to dissect and establish the relations, structures and interactions which impinge upon them. The interplay between practices, policies and actors should be the focal point of social analyses. By no means can change be achieved unless we identify and challenge the 'interactive framework' within which inclusive policies are embedded (Squipp, 1981).

Educational policy is defined as a political struggle implicated in a multidimensional and interactive network comprising both structures and actors. A constitutive element of this network is the notion of ideology, which, if examined from a critical perspective, is directly implicated in the interplay of unequal power relations emanating both from agency and structure.

Central to analyzing ideology in terms of power relations is language. Language is a pervasive means of power that is materialized through discourse and permeates both actors and structures. The analysis of ideology, therefore, should include the ways in which ideology is materialized and embodied within the institutional infrastructure of a particular socio-political system. The discursive constitution of reality is a pervasive means of power that renders the processes and outcomes of educational policymaking an essentially political issue. What follows in the next chapter is an attempt to investigate the ways in which ideologies are materialized through the institutional infrastructure of a particular socio-political system, and bring to bear a profound impact on the ways that special education policies are conceptualized and enacted.

Useful Websites

Discourse in Society
   www.discourses.org/
Theory and Practice in Critical Discourse Analysis
   http://gseis.ucla.edu/faculty/kellner/ed270/Luke/SAHA6.html

6

Inclusive Policies and Institutional Conditions

Introduction

This chapter examines the institutional embodiments of ideologies that have an important impact on the processes and outcomes of inclusive education policymaking. The institutional conditions (e.g., legislation, economic and administrative conditions) endemic to a socio-political context can have a huge impact on the ways in which educational policy is conceptualized and enacted, thus facilitating or undermining the realization of an inclusive discourse. The competing ideas and interpretations, which are at play during the processes of educational policymaking, constitute the 'politics of inclusion' that are significantly influenced by dominant ideologies and their institutional ramifications.

The chapter provides a critical exploration of the ways in which constitutional and legislative conditions, administrative-political and bureaucratic conditions, along with economic conditions, influence the process of policy constitution and implementation. Relevant snapshots from different countries will also be provided in order to apply abstract theoretical ideas to practice.

As we have already seen in Chapter 4, inclusive education policymaking is part of an interactive process and, evidently, there is always a widespread tension and conflict inherent in this particular terrain, as a plethora of political, ideological and social influences are at work (Lunt, 1998). The competing ideas and interpretations which underpin inclusive education policymaking are immensely influenced by different discourses, as well as by the socio-economic structure of a given society (Shapiro, 1980; Squip, 1984). Within this interactive framework the politics of inclusion are defined in multiple and even contradictory ways, and render the struggles towards the realization of an inclusive discourse a rather strenuous exercise, both in conceptual and practical terms.

The institutional conditions can have profound implications for the ways in which educational policy is conceptualized and acted upon (Fulcher, 1999), thus enhancing or undermining the attempts made within all arenas of the educational apparatus to foster greater inclusive policies and practices. Given the multidimensional character of educational change, during the interplays of power relations 'many institutionalised routines continue to be reproduced even during the most radical episodes of change' (Cohen, 1989: 46), an assertion that points to the significant influence of institutional infrastructure over any transformative attempts that social actors might undertake. Social actors alone cannot thus bring change unless the institutional infrastructure of a socio-political system is favourably positioned towards these changes.

Institutional conditions occasionally prevent social actors from being the prime agents of change, as they cannot engage in rational decision making within organizations and provide a thorough and comprehensive examination of alternatives, along with the potential consequences that may ensue (Mehan, 1984). As earlier discussed in Chapter 5, the actions of social actors and the alternatives these might entail are constricted by the dominant institutional, legislative and administrative regimes.

Given the multiplicity of accounts and perspectives that are interlinked with, and impact upon, the policymaking process, inclusive education policy analysis necessitates a thorough understanding of the institutional conditions that are at play during this process. According to Carlson (2005: 149), '. . . it is imperative to consider how contemporary practices and institutions . . . shape the lines that are drawn between "disabled" and "nondisabled"'.

Towards this end, the next section outlines the ways in which institutional conditions are implicated in the policymaking process. The analysis will be based upon Fulcher's (1999) taxonomy of institutional conditions, which is as follows: (a) Constitutional, (b) Legislative, (c) Administrative-political and bureaucratic and (d) Economic. It needs noting, however, that one cannot establish a clear demarcation line between these conditions as they overlap and are interrelated.

Constitutional and legislative conditions

Instances of power are manifested in the dominant discourses enshrined in official legislation of nation states. As Scott (1990: 58) suggests: 'Many of the most important public documents form a part of a system of surveillance and social control that have become such an integral part of bureaucratic nation states.' Even though educational policymaking cannot be confined within the governmental terrain, the constitutional and legislative conditions of a nation state can immensely, even though not deterministically, influence the ways in which inclusive education policies are conceptualized and acted upon. As Slee and Cook (1999: 67) write: '. . . of itself the Law is not capable of eliminating disability discrimination. Paradoxically, the Law can be enlisted as a tactic for disablement or enablement.' In much the same way, Barton (2008b: 10) asserts that 'The question of how to prevent discrimination and exclusion does raise the issue of the nature and function of legislation in this process of development. While legislation is not sufficient in itself to produce inclusion, it is a necessary factor in the process of change.'

Social policy imperatives (Daniels, 2000) can also exert a dynamic role in policy constitution and dissemination. For example, the introduction of the Warnock Report in England (DfES, 1978) was the direct result of a general advocacy of social policy towards greater equality and a pronounced emphasis upon disabled and other disadvantaged members of the society (Lunt, 1998). Arguably, a human rights perspective can effectively enhance the role of the government in protecting the personal autonomy and welfare of its citizens.

Riddell et al. (2000), drawing on the work of Kirp (1982) and Mashaw (1983), provide an insightful account of the salient special education policy frameworks that have been in existence in England and Scotland. In particular they refer to the bureaucratic, professional and legal policy frameworks which co-exist and are dynamically interrelated. The choice of the dominant policy framework is indicative of the ways in which special education is defined and conceptualized.

For instance, legislative developments couched in assimilationist and compensatory models of educational support, fail to address the discriminatory and disabling processes of the wider society, and place squarely the emphasis on disabled students' individual pathology. Campbell (2005: 113) discusses the 'exacting and explicit role' of the Law in the 'subjectifying activity of the government' 'by allocating and regulating populations into fixed ontological categories (such as disability, gender, sex and race, thereby foregrounding the fixed, transcendental and, hence, apolitical nature of disability)'. By implication, it is suggested that it is important to make transparent the 'subjectifying activity' of State policy that is firmly embedded in 'biomedical technologies and ascriptions' (Campbell, 2005: 113), notwithstanding the 'textual manoeuvres that give a gloss of coherence, consensus and commonsense in a collection of mutually contradictory educational fantasies' (MacLure, 1994: 285).

Armstrong et al. (2010: 92) argue that the disability legislation introduced by the New Labour Government in England fails to articulate disability as a social construct and as 'an act of discrimination embedded in the power relations of society'. In particular, the Disability Discrimination Act, 1995 (House of Commons, 1995) and the Special Educational Needs and Disability Act (DfES, 2001) are predominantly informed by the medical model of disability (Howie, 2010). In this respect:

> The wider social question of why discrimination and disadvantage are so embedded in the system is lost in legislation that represents inclusion in terms of 'impairment friendly' schooling. Similarly, there is no consideration of how the relations of power that support discrimination against disabled people can be transformed as a necessary basis for an inclusive society. (Armstrong et al., 2010: 92)

In a parallel way, Norwich (2010) comments on the definition of SEN adopted by the SEN Code of Practice (DfES, 2001) for England and Wales, whereby the document fails to conjure up the notion of SEN as being firmly embedded in and resulting from the interstices of class, socio-economic status and ethnicity. In much the same way, the recent SEN Green Paper (DfE, 2011b: 14), which allegedly represents 'a new approach to special educational needs and disability', is significantly imbued by a deficit-oriented perspective in terms of its assessment procedures that locate the 'problem' within the individuals concerned.

> Disabled children and children with SEN experience a wide range of barriers because of physical and sensory impairments, learning difficulties such as dyslexia, or a variety of needs. (DfE, 2011b: 14)

Constitutional conditions are also important in safeguarding and reinstating disabled individuals' human rights. Rothstein and Johnson (2010) refer to two judicial interpretations of the fourteenth amendment of the United States Constitution. These interpretations pointed to the fact that even though the:

> District of Columbia and the Commonwealth of Pennsylvania provided education to children within their jurisdictions, they were denying due process and equal protection to children with disabilities by excluding these children from the educational system. (Rothstein and Johnson, 2010: 6)

In order to assist states to respond to the constitutional requirements with regard to the education of disabled students, the Congress inaugurated a federal program of subsidization.

Moreover, the active role that the US federal courts play in educational policymaking is stressed, in the sense that they are concerned with the fundamental rights of disabled students, as these are represented by the constitutional requirements of the State. Hayes (1984) (cited in Fulcher, 1999) regards the courts and the development of administrative law as critical sites through which the rights of disabled children can be reinstated. These rights include, among other things, protection against discrimination. For instance, court cases in the United States of America have addressed, 'questions about whether certain groups of children (behaviourally disordered . . . learning disabled) are being appropriately identified' (Rothstein and Johnson, 2010: 90).

In England and Wales, the introduction of the Special Educational Needs and Disability Tribunal (SENDisT) allows parents of children designated as having special educational needs to appeal against decisions made by local authorities. The Special Educational Needs Tribunal was established in 1994, but in 2002 it inaugurated new procedures concerned with claims for disability discrimination and it was renamed the Special Educational Needs and Disability Tribunal (SENDisT). Even though tribunals have empowered parents to pursue their disabled children's rights through litigation, parents' experiences of going to SENDisT suggest that the process is time consuming, expensive and emotionally wrecking (Runswick-Cole, 2007).

In terms of legislative conditions, particular consideration should also be given to 'disjointed incrementalism' or 'incremental dissonance' of policy which, according to Loxley and Thomas (1997: 277), refers to the 'accretion of policy, as opposed to its strategic development'. In other words, new policies or new covenants are being introduced, which far from being complementary to the existing ones, are, in essence, antithetical. Loxley and Thomas (2001: 299) provide the following succinct observation:

> What is happening is the layering of new policies that have a notional objective 'inclusion', on top of practices that have demonstrably contrary effects. An ungenerous observer might suggest that the government is trying to have its cake and eat it.

Similarly, while exploring the sustainability of Inclusive School Reform in Florida, USA, Sindelar et al. (2006) discuss the ways in which certain changes in state and district policies undermined a particular school's process of sustainable inclusive school reform. As they write:

> Redefining success on the basis of academic test performance obscured the benefits of inclusion, particularly for students with disabilities and other students with learning difficulties, and thus undermined the sustainability of the reform. (Sindelar et al., 2006: 329–30)

The emergence of contradictory policies by the governmental terrain poses profound moral and ideological dilemmas which confound policy and adversely affect the implementation process. As Armstrong et al. (2000: 74) poignantly put it, the 'contradictory relationships between policies have confused and interrupted the attempts to introduce change'.

Conflict theories in education intended to explore relations of domination, authority, coercion and compliance of some groups to others (Tomlinson, 1982: 17) assume a crucial role in revealing and explaining the contradictions and inconsistencies that are inherent in the governmental terrain, as the State tries to promote inclusion and simultaneously to preserve the status quo. This is what Habermas (1973) calls 'the crisis of legitimacy'. According to Tomlinson (1982: 105), 'A crisis comes about when a system, in this case an education system, cannot rationally or politically meet the ideological commitments needed to maintain legitimacy'. In effect, the conflict between egalitarian ideologies and social and economic interests is manifested in inclusive educational policies. The vestiges of special educational thinking, and the intrusion of market forces in education, undermine initiatives to promote an inclusive discourse. In other words, the existence of contradictory policies along with the ambivalent considerations that saturate certain policies constitute great impediments to the realization of an inclusive discourse (Wedell, 2005). Wedell (2008: 128), while analyzing the institutional and legislative changes that took place in the UK context in favour of inclusion, points out that

> It is evident that those schools that are successful in implementing inclusion achieve this despite the system, rather than because of it. In other words, the occurrence of 'good practice' does not validate the existing system.

Reflective Exercise

Think of recent legislative developments in your context and discuss the extent to which they promote or hinder aspects of inclusive education.

Administrative-political and bureaucratic conditions

Legislation can be interpreted in varied ways and, therefore, the ensuing administrative-political and bureaucratic practices can be regarded as being relatively independent from any legislative decisions. Having said that, however, we should not undermine the influential role of legislation on these practices (Fulcher, 1999). Recent changes, for instance, in the Individuals with Disabilities Act in the United States of America have been the result of criticisms over the ways in which the Act brought, according to Rothstein and Johnson (2010: 349), 'unnecessary bureaucracy, paperwork, and costs to public education'. In the United Kingdom, the recent SEN Green Paper (DfE, 2011) stipulates the necessity of reducing the bureaucracy around the SEN statementing process that resulted from the SEN Code of Practice (DfES, 2001).

Bureaucracy has become an 'iron cage' and, hence, a powerful means of exerting control on people in irreversible ways (Weber, 1952; 1968). Lingard et al. (2005: 774) draw upon the work of Bourdieu (1996a) in order to highlight the highly structured and static nature of bureaucracies and their pervasive impact on policy development and implementation. Special education professionals are in a way the new bureaucrats or technocrats who invoke 'the universal' as a means to wield their power in unobtrusive ways. Their personal decisions and impositions are masqueraded under the realm of 'neutrality', 'expertise' and the ethics of 'public service'.

The discourse of professionalism is 'institutionally sanctioned' (Brantlinger, 1997: 432) and, therefore, is immensely powerful and pervasive within all contexts of special educational policy and practice, whereby 'unequal power relations' are established and sustained (Thompson, 1984). As Tomlinson (1985: 163) has argued, the notion of special educational needs has become an 'ideological rationalisation for those who have the power to shape and define the expanding special education system'.

Recently there have been concerns over the ways in which the role of the Special Educational Needs Coordinator (SENCO) in the United Kingdom is occasionally reduced to an administrative and bureaucratic level (Mackenzie, 2007; Szwed 2007; Pearson, 2010). The bureaucratic nature of the statutory framework on SEN is well documented (DfES, 2004; DfE, 2011), and prevents SENCOs from fulfilling 'their main tasks relating to children's learning' (Szwed, 2007: 97). Cole (2005: 288) highlights the necessity to proceed to the 'reprofessionalization' of SENCOs, with a view to enabling them to become 'powerful and reflective practitioners who could be in a position to take on the mantle of inclusion within mainstream schools'. Towards this end, SENCOs need to (re) conceptualize their role as being/becoming agents of change within the context of inclusion (Liasidou and Svensson, 2011). The 'reprofessionalization' of SENCOs role should be mobilized by a policy reform agenda intended to initiate:

> a move towards ways of determining impact and effectiveness and away from an emphasis on the SENCO being solely responsible for the burdensome, bureaucratic demands of the special educational needs Code, thereby enabling SENCOs to have sufficient time to carry out the central tasks of delivering pedagogical and curriculum interventions. (Mackenzie, 2007: 217)

The introduction of the Education (Special Educational Needs Coordinators) (England) (Amendment) Regulations (2009) – is concerned with ensuring that new SENCOs undertake a nationally approved training to obtain the National Award for Special Educational Needs Coordination – with a view to reconfiguring their professional role and status. The new role envisaged in the National Award for SEN Coordination (TDA, 2009) necessitates a shift from bureaucratic and managerial considerations to a more strategic approach to removing barriers to learning and initiating an inclusive education reform agenda.

Apart from the aforesaid institutional conditions, we should not underestimate other institutional conditions, because even though they are not directly related to special education they can have a major impact on it. For instance, it is well documented that there is a very close and reciprocal relationship between poverty and disability, because people living in poverty are more likely to become disabled (Elwan, 1999; Milttler, 1999; DCSF, 2009a). Hence, an effective health care system that is accessible to people across different socio-economic backgrounds can potentially minimize disability and dependency. Turnbull (2009) regards the health care system as an important human service system that is directly linked to special education. As he writes, 'Special Education links to it [health care system] because children who are not born healthy, raised in healthy homes, nourished well, and who are denied effective early intervention and do not receive robust medical treatment become special education students' (Turnbull, 2009: 7).

Bureaucratic consideration can also be analyzed in relation to the role of parents of disabled children, who are disempowered by official legislative arrangements and bureaucratic procedures underpinning special and inclusive education (Armstrong, 1995; Duncan, 2003). Despite suggesting that some parents can be more powerful and assertive than others, MacBeath et al. (2006: 55) highlight the fact that even in these cases, parents 'had learned painfully through dealing with bureaucracies to make demands and not to take no for an answer . . .' Understandably, even for those powerful and more assertive parents, it is still the case that they have to strive for their children's entitlements and challenge disempowering legislative and bureaucratic procedures. The Lamb Enquiry (DCFS, 2009d) in the United Kingdom pointed to the need to improve parental confidence in special educational needs after exploring parents' experiences of the SEN provision, statutory assessment and the issuing of a statement.

Economic conditions

Economic conditions play a fundamental role in shaping policy and practice with regard to disability and special educational needs. The restructuring of capital and the increase of profits presuppose that policy imperatives should be primarily concerned with enhancing effectiveness and efficiency within schools. As we have seen in Chapter 5, under the siege of neo-liberal ideologies, the aim is to enhance the standards in classrooms and preserve social order for the benefit, however, of those who are perceived as being 'ideal students', and have the potential to advance the educational outcomes of schools at a minimum cost. The above considerations raise concerns regarding the competitive nature of different policies for scarce resources. Some policies are more resourced than others and there is no doubt that the standards agenda is well resourced while the inclusion agenda is not (Barton and Armstrong, 2007).

Professionals (e.g., teachers, educational psychologists) can be characterized as gatekeepers of the State's scarce financial resources. As a result, they are used by the State to legitimate exclusionary practices within schools in favour of either the maintenance of the class and social relations status quo or in favour of the 'commodification of education and the child' (Ball, 2004b: 13). The presence of disabled students in mainstream schools is regarded as being a counterforce to attempts to achieve excellent results in high stakes testing and subsequent league table rankings, and as a result 'the "ideal student" becomes a source of educational aspiration' (Harwood and Humphy, 2008: 380) while disabled individuals are marginalized and excluded in a system that prioritizes and values the 'perfomative worth of individuals' (Ball, 2009: 42).

Economic conditions should also be examined in more pragmatic terms, namely in terms of the ways in which the State offers sufficient economic resources in order to promote inclusive policies. Notwithstanding the fact that economic conditions do not determinate policy and practice at other levels of the educational apparatus, they can considerably influence the patterns of provision and models of delivery deployed and the extent to which they promote or hinder inclusion. Peter (1998) points to the crucial role that adequate resourcing plays in promoting inclusive education practices. As he contends: 'it should remind the architects of any anticipated legislation that, without properly resourced support, this inclusive initiative may well prove at best empty if elegant rhetoric . . .' (Peter, 1998: 13).

Nevertheless, notwithstanding their importance, economic conditions should not deflect attention from other more crucial considerations concerned with the necessity to proceed to fundamental educational and ideological change in alignment with the tenets of an inclusive discourse (Slee, 1993; Vlachou, 1997). As Turnbull (2009: 6) writes while discussing the current USA special education legislative framework: 'No doubt, more money would be helpful, especially if it were better spent (such as on RTI, school-wide positive behaviour support, universal design of the curriculum and workforce capacity building). But more than money is needed'.

Evans (2007) suggests that the ways in which special education is funded has major implications for effective development of provision and delivery of services. Research has concentrated on exploring the ways in which 'mechanisms of financing special education can explain discrepancies between policy intentions and practical outcomes' (Fletcher-Cambell, 2002: 19). These considerations also raise issues over the equal distribution of resources. Taking as an example the UK context, notwithstanding research evidence suggesting increase in overall funding in inclusive and special education, there are significant inequalities resulting from the amount of resources allocated (Terzi, 2010).

Moreover, the question of economic conditions necessitates exploring the main funding formulae adopted by various educational systems and identifying the principles underpinning them (Parrish, 2000; Marsh, 2003; Evans, 2007). Graham (2005), for instance, discusses the Education Adjustment Program (EAP) in Queensland Education, Australia, that is used as a resourcing methodology in Special and Inclusive Education. Even though the launch of EAP was supposed 'to facilitate the placement and resourcing of children with recognised disabilities within the mainstream', it still 'retains disability categories' and has relied upon a needs-based approach that draws heavily on 'medical diagnosis and descriptions of impairment' (Graham, 2005: 11). This mode of funding is based on what Slee (2011: 123) calls 'The bureaucratic discourse that focuses on the diagnosis of disability as a lever for delivering resources to individual students'. This kind of discourse, '. . . establishes very limited notions of identity. People are 'anatomised', reduced to the anatomical features of what is described as their syndrome or disorder . . . [and] conceal social dysfunction and disorder . . .' (ibid.).

As a response to a predominance of bureaucratic discourses in resource allocation, Evans (2007) writes that patterns of budgetary school provision should be utilized in flexible ways and be premised on a more holistic approach to children's needs. In so doing it will be possible 'to ensure the most effective approach for each child, and the issue of funding will be less focused on individuals and more on curriculum delivery across teaching groups' (Evans, 2007: 53). Promoting greater inclusive policy and practice also necessitates devising decentralizing systems of resourcing, characterized by seamless and simplified communications channels that can ensure 'value for money'. The latter is exemplified in terms of the extent to which budgetary allocation concentrates on providing direct input for students with special educational needs, rather than for administrative, diagnostic and litigation procedures (Fletcher-Cambell, 2002: 19).

Deconstructing legislation: deconstructing unequal power relations

Even though educational policy is diffused within all arenas of the educational apparatus, it is within governmental terrain that the context of influence and the subsequent context of text production are conceptualized and materialized through the formal policy documents. The 'diffusion' of policy, therefore, is circumscribed within the parameters set by the State, without however eschewing the possibility that new and antithetical versions of formal policy can be manifested within the context of practice. As Ball (1993: 13) writes,

> Textual interventions can change things significantly, but I am suggesting that we should not ignore the ways that things stay the same nor the ways in which changes are different in different settings and different from the intentions of policy authors (where these are clear).

Thus, 'Policies do not normally tell you what to do; they create circumstance in which the range of options available in deciding what to do are narrowed or changed' (Ball, 1993: 12). The conceptualization of policy as text, which can be characterized as a celebration of 'human potentiality', as the text can be interpreted in multifarious ways, is obliterated by the policy as discourse, which sets the discursive frame within which agents within all arenas can be actively engaged in the policymaking process. As discussed in Chapter 5, Ball (1993) inaugurates and talks extensively about the policy as discourse that goes beyond and simultaneously saturates the policy as text. The struggles that are inherent in educational policymaking process are thus according to Ball (1993: 15) 'set within a moving discursive frame which articulates and constrains the possibilities and probabilities of interpretation and enactment'. The discourses that constitute this frame emanate from those with institutional 'power' who are the bearers of the 'agentic marshalling of discourse' (Bacchi, 2000: 52).

In this respect, it is evident that 'Policy-makers' assumptions – along with those of other significant political actors – set limits on the alternatives considered feasible for policy implementation' (Jenson, 1997: 294; cited in Bacchi, 2000: 53), as they construe and disseminate 'domains of objects and rituals of truth' (Foucault, 1979b: 194). Policy formulation is thus inevitably subject to intense discursive power struggles in order to 'construct (a sense of) reality and to circulate that reality as widely and smoothly as possible throughout society' (Fiske, 1989: 150; cited in Apple, 2000: 43). This being the case, it is important to identify the dominant discourses that constitute this frame (Ball, 1993; Bacchi, 2000), while concomitantly exposing the unequal power relations or the technologies of power (Foucault, 1977a) that are at work in the policymaking process.

While acknowledging that the role of discourse analysis should not be limited to the analysis of texts in educational policy, it is primarily within this analysis that the 'spatial shifting' (Armstrong, 2003) of disabled children initially emerges. This spatial shifting is covertly expressed through the various discourses that surface within the official policy documents and are implicated within asymmetrical power relations. The 'state's autocratic streak' (Evans, 1994: 62) is initially reflected within its official policy documents that are littered with hegemonic and pervasive discourses, that constitute and are constituted by unequal power relations, that as Bacchi (2000: 54) writes 'leave the power to define "need" and "disadvantage" in those designing the policy', thus bringing in the frontline of educational policy analysis the 'dangerous and debilitating conceits of official discourse' (Humes and Bryce, 2003: 179). These official policy documents are, in essence, 'an expression of sets of political intentions and a political resource for continual national debates . . .' (Ball and Bowe, 1992: 100) with far reaching consequences for special educational policy and practice.

The moral dimension of educational policy analysis seeks to expose and analyse the ways in which less powerful groups of people are systematically subjected to political, social and institutional dehumanizing impositions, which are represented as naturalized and legitimized processes. Fulcher (1999), for instance, provides an insightful account of the ways in which asymmetrical power relations, or the politics of disablement (Oliver, 1990), are evidenced in educational policies and practices that lead to the marginalization and spatial exclusion of disabled people. Similarly, Armstrong (2003: 26) analyzes the ways in which power relations act as a 'social quarantine' (Foucault, 1977a) through which disabled people are 'spatially shifted and placed outside the mainstream'. The discourses inscribed in these policies constitute a kind of unassailable knowledge which privileges those who hold institutional power, since power and knowledge become indispensable.

An important task, therefore, is to investigate the knowledge upon which special education policy is based and expose the ways that this knowledge is arbitrarily constructed, thus constituting a corrosive means for the exertion of power. This knowledge is produced and concurrently produces power, thus creating a circle of domination and imposition. So central is power to the constitution of knowledge that Foucault accords primacy to power rather than knowledge. Thus, for Foucault (1977a: 27), 'There is no power relation without the correlative constitution of a field of knowledge, nor any knowledge that does not presuppose and constitute at the same time, power relations.'

Throughout these processes of spatialization, the various issues get, as Bacchi (2000: 46) writes, 'represented in ways that mystify power relations and often create individuals responsible for their "failures", drawing attention away from the structures that create unequal outcomes'. The pervasiveness of these 'mystified' discourses, and the asymmetrical power relations that emanate from them, are relayed to the institutions within which policies are implemented. These discourses are subsequently regenerated and reconfigured within institutions, whereby the power relations are materialized and reconstituted. These unequal power relations are eventually legitimized, thus perpetuating a cycle of domination and subordination.

This cycle can be challenged only when deconstruction extends beyond the text, to the deconstruction of social and cultural processes that are evinced through 'representations in films and the media, and the built environment, the effects of legislation and embedded social practices . . .' (Armstrong, 2003: 73). The dismantling process should emerge from a top-down perspective, thus initially leading to a 'demystification process' of the powerful discourses and unequal power relations that are inscribed within the official policy documents. The road towards inclusion is fraught with unequal confrontations between the dubious 'neutrality' of State and disabled people, whose empowerment is paradoxically debilitated by that from which it should have emerged: the Welfare State.

Summary

This chapter has been given over to the investigation of the institutional infrastructure underpinning inclusive education policy constitution and dissemination, and explored the discursive contours imposed by the institutional infrastructure through which ideologies are infiltrated, reified and regenerated. The material existence of ideologies and their reification through the institutional conditions of a socio-political system have a profound impact on policy constitution and dissemination.

It is occasionally the case that institutional conditions impede social actors from being the prime agents of change, as they cannot engage in rational decision making within organizations and provide a thorough and spherical examination of alternatives along with the potential consequences these might have. Put differently, the actions of social actors and the alternatives these might entail are delimited by the various discourses that permeate institutions.

Special attention has been given to the pervasiveness of official legislation and its delimiting effects on practice. The metaphor of 'policy as discourse' sets conceptual and pragmatic confinements to the implementation process. It is occasionally the case that legislative documents are essentially littered with hegemonic and subjugating discourses that constitute, and concomitantly are constituted by, unequal power relations. The pervasiveness of these 'mystified' discourses, and the asymmetrical power relations immanent in them, are relayed to the various institutions whereby policies are inserted, thereby confounding policy implementation.

Reflective Exercise

Think of a number of institutional conditions (within your country/context of practice) that undermine attempts to foster greater inclusive policies and practices.

In what ways do contradictory policies undermine attempts to foster greater inclusive policies and practices?

Useful Websites

European Agency for Development in Special Needs Education

www.european-agency.org/

Results-INCLUDE-ED integrated project from Sixth Framework Programme

www.ub.edu/includ-ed/results.htm

7

Cross-Cultural Perspectives on Inclusive Education Policymaking

Introduction

The chapter highlights the importance of adopting a comparative per-spective in policy analysis, and discusses issues of policy borrowing and neo-colonialism. The critical dimension of policy studies involves, among other things, a context-specific approach to questioning and destabiliz-ing culturally grounded inequalities of power and hierarchical subject positions that give rise to exclusionary practices and subjugating regimes. This is part of providing the 'bigger picture' (Grace, 1991) of inclusive edu-cation policymaking across different geopolitical contexts, and explor-ing the ways in which a pluralistic framework of complex and contesting values underpinning the processes and outcomes of inclusive education policymaking can be devised and acted upon in culturally and historically informed ways.

Globalization and inclusion: the dialectic of the global and the local

Cross-cultural research in relation to inclusion is crucial in documenting the highly political nature of the notion, as well as in making transparent the host of contextual dynamics influencing the processes of inclusive education policymaking (Barton and Armstrong, 2007). Barton and Tomlinson (1984) pointed to the dearth of comparative sociological analyses pertaining to disability and SEN, an observation that acted as 'a really prophetic advisory note to future authors' (Daniels and Garner, 1999: 7; cited in Barton, 2003: 3). The internationalization of analyses with regard to disability and SEN has been instrumental in making transparent the multiple and diverse dynamics impacting on the processes and outcomes of special and inclusive education policymaking (Armstrong and Barton, 1999, 2000; Barton and Armstrong, 2007).

It is extremely useful to learn about the variegated contextual sociopolitical and historical frameworks against which the struggles for inclusive education (Vlachou, 1997) are taking place, and to acquire a cross-cultural understanding of inclusion. In so doing, it will be possible to reflect on our own policies and practices and be enabled to 'think otherwise' (Ball, 1998), thereby addressing the highly political nature of inclusion. As Barton and Armstrong (2007: 1) write:

> We cannot underestimate the importance of recognizing the particularities, as well as the commonalities, of some of the priorities, barriers and contradictions involved in trying to widen participation in education in different settings. It is very clear that we cannot just apply the language of 'inclusion' uncritically, assuming that meanings will be shared across cultures – or even within the same national context or educational authority.

Notwithstanding globalization and the ease in which policies travel across cultures through systematic or ad hoc networks of dissemination (Levin, 1998), local powerful policymakers, namely politicians and officials, are not so much concerned with the specificities of these policies, but they are more likely, as Halpin and Troyna (1995: 306) comment, 'to be interested in a borrowed policy's political symbolism than its details'. This phenomenon is more prominent in countries where policymakers are forced to introduce educational changes (Nguyen et al., 2009).

Thus, in spite of a certain degree of homogeneity among countries with regard to the discursive impediments looming over the attempts to foster greater inclusive policies '[d]ifferent historical conditions posit different problems and demand a range of diverse solutions' (Giroux, 2003: 5). This is precisely why cross-cultural analyses of disability and special educational needs are necessary, in order to trace the provenance of a host of exclusionary discourses that discreetly permeate not only the official policy documents but also the whole political and social edifice of a nation-state. As Foucault (1980: 131) writes, 'Each society has its regime of truth, its general politics of truth: that is, the types of discourse which it accepts and makes function as true.'

Thus, in spite of the overarching influence of globalization, it is evident, according to Dale (1999: 3) that 'the effects of globalization are mediated, in both directions and in complex ways, by existing national patterns and structures . . .' Understandably, the political discourse is infiltrated or even reshaped according to policymakers' own motives, interests, aspirations, values and beliefs and according to the local historical and political exigencies. Ball (2009: 31) suggests that, in policy analysis it is important to understand the ways in which '. . . [Policies] interact with, interrupt or conflict with other policies in play in national and local settings and with long-standing indigenous policy traditions to produce particular versions and mediations of policy.'

It is, therefore, necessary to adopt a cross-cultural perspective and interrogate the ways that the 'cultural politics' of inclusive education policymaking are played out, contested and manifested within distinct socio-political contexts. If we are genuinely interested in inclusive policies we should seek to dissect and establish the relations, structures and interactions which impinge upon them. The interplay among contextual practices, policies and actors should be the focal point of social analysis.

Cross-cultural research can take many forms according to the focal point of analysis. It can concentrate on single national case studies, and it may be either descriptive or explorative. The explorative case study utilizes a critical approach and investigates the ideological, political and cultural underpinnings of educational policymaking, thereby providing a holistic outlook in exploring a host of culturally and historically grounded dynamics impacting on the policymaking process.

This kind of cross-cultural research can be simultaneously comparative, in the sense that it can compare different historical periods within a particular socio-political context (Sweeting, 2001; Watson, 2001). This would bring to the

surface the incessant struggles over meaning and over the historical and contextual dimensions of policy constitution and dissemination. The historical
dimension of cross-cultural research is an extremely important task (Arnove,
2003) in attempting to disassemble the contentious and, thereby, political
nature of inclusion and lay bare its interconnectedness with issues of human
rights and social justice within particular historical periods. Gale (2001: 385)
explores different ways of conducting critical policy analysis and explains the
ways in which policy historiography can be *specifically* applied (policy genealogy can be also utilized for this purpose) in order to portray 'substantive issues
of policy at particular hegemonic moments', with a view to mapping the process of educational change and making transparent the possible relationships
'between the socio-political present and the socio-political past'.

That said, inclusive education policy analysis should not be limited to
a synchronic analysis of the macro and micro dynamics impacting on the
policymaking process, but it should also be concerned with exploring the
ways in which these dynamics have come into being (diachronic analysis).
A diachronic analysis can trace their historical provenance, as well as their
overarching impact on today's interactive network of policy constitution and
dissemination (Liasidou, 2008b, 2009). Diachronic dynamics might be subtle
and inconspicuous, but they are rather pervasive and corrosive because they
have become naturalized and thereby sacred. A diachronic analysis 'defamil-
iarizes the present as much as it makes us familiar with a forgotten past. The
point is to create distance from ourselves, to see the contingency of what may
otherwise seem natural and inevitable' (Allen, 2005: 102).

Taking as an example the case of Cyprus, the failure to promote inclusion
can be partly attributed to the historical past of the island (Liasidou, 2008b;
Symeonidou, 2009). Considerable evidence suggests that disabled children
are systematically relegated to the margins of a hostile educational system
(Angelides, 2004; Phtiaka, 2006; Liasidou, 2007). This is not surprising, if we
take into consideration the ways in which issues of human rights and equality are perceived and acted upon in an island that has long been bedevilled by
colonialism and has struggled to preserve its national integrity. As a result of
these historical conjunctures:

> Cyprus is still struggling to establish a strong democratic tradition and thereby lacks
> a focus on human rights issues and equality. As a result there is also as Mavratsas
> (2003) contends, an underdeveloped citizenship and by implication, a lack of plu-
> ralism and tolerability that consolidates the 'preservation of the prevalent political

practice and the wider status quo' (p. 53). The excessive nationalism undermines the notion of the citizen and the person, and embraces the existence of 'ideological monopolies', something that impedes the development of pluralism and cultural politics, which go beyond the oppressive connotations that the word tolerance might imply (Slee, 2003) . . . Not surprisingly, the rejection of the other, the intolerability to difference and diversity are against the emancipatory attempts towards the realization of an inclusive discourse. (Liasidou, 2008b: 235)

An acknowledgement of the temporal and contextual nature of inclusion will open new possibilities in fostering an inclusive discourse. Change possibilities can be feasible only when we are aware of the context and time-specific 'discursive contours' within which policy agendas are conceptualized and implemented, the aim being to unravel and 'trace the process of educational change and to expose the possible relationships between the socio-political present and the socio-political past' (Gale, 2001: 385). According to Arnove (2003: 7–8):

If understanding is to be advanced as to what works and does not work in a country, then such study must be guided by knowledge of that country, by familiarity with the history and unique qualities, . . . of the forces and attitudes governing its social organizations, of the political and economic conditions that determine its developments.

Occasionally, local dynamics are axiomatically incompatible with the tenets of inclusion and are consequently complicit in the ascendancy of contradictory and contentious policy landscapes that reduce inclusion to a special education artefact. The pursuit of emancipatory change (Barton, 2005) necessitates understanding and problematizing a vast array of culturally grounded and historically rooted power/knowledge relations that produce the normative assumptions and orthodoxies underpinning the policymaking process. In so doing it will be possible to understand the origins of some of the exclusionary discourses that undermine inclusion. At the same time, it would be possible to decipher the ways in which these discursive dynamics have been engendered, contested, negotiated, sustained and proliferated, thereby reinforcing and perpetuating special education imperatives, notwithstanding rhetoric around inclusion.

Sharing useful knowledge presupposes a clear and comprehensive understanding of inclusive education across different contexts. The contextual dimensions of inclusive education policymaking can provide effective local responses to the challenges in fostering greater inclusive policies and practices, and can inform cross-cultural debates on the commonalities and idiosyncrasies of different localities, along with the ways in which ideas are conceptualized, interpreted and acted upon. Constructive dialogue among academics, policymakers and practitioners, both within and between countries, can provide the platform for dealing with similar challenges and devising quality education programmes responsive to learner diversity. As Barton (2008a: xix) writes: 'Within our own work contexts and societies there is so much that is unacceptable and exclusionary and needs to be fought over and changed and we must be part of the critical engagement'. It is in this respect that Lingard and Mills (2007: 237), while providing an analysis of pedagogy, point to the necessity of trusting teachers' professionalism and their ability to infiltrate research literature 'through a careful reading of the demands and specificities of their students, classes, locale, and space of nation and globe'.

Even though there are no recipes and 'magic fixes' prescribing the ways in which inclusive educational policies can be formulated and enacted across the globe, there are certain 'rules' that are indispensable in the pursuit of an inclusive discourse, and can constitute the conceptual and theoretical backdrop against which the struggles for greater inclusive policy and practice should take place. As Barton and Armstrong (2007: 4) suggest, in spite of the fact that 'there is no one history of inclusive education . . . , there is an international purpose behind those struggling and supporting inclusion'.

As a corollary to the above considerations, the realization of an inclusive discourse necessitates the existence of a clear and unambiguous purpose and vision that will concentrate on the identification and effacement of the variegated hurdles that impinge upon fostering greater inclusive policies and practices. The process of change is a localized struggle embroiled in an intricate web of interdependencies and consequential effects. In this sense, the process of change is not perceived as a 'uniform abstraction' (Foucault, 1978: 24) that can be easily achieved through facile political rhetoric and unidimensional perspectives. Change, according to progressive politics, comes through the accumulation of a profusion of macro and micro discursive 'ruptures' that embody 'possibilities for transformation and the play of dependencies between those transformations' (Foucault cited in Macey, 1994: xix) at local and global levels. Hence, even the tiniest locus of resistance in all arenas of educational policymaking can have a massive impact on mobilizing transformative change. At the same time, however, this theoretical stance highlights that change is not necessary to be a revolutionary or a one-off attempt in order to be effective. Inclusion is a slow and demanding process and, hence, every little attempt is significant and contributes to the gradual construction of more inclusive educational policies and practices.

Reflective Exercise

How do you understand the historically and culturally grounded character of inclusion?

What aspects of your socio-political context need to be addressed in order to foster greater inclusive policy and practice?

Policy borrowing in inclusive education

Inclusion constitutes a globalizing discourse and, as a result, it has also been subjected to the distorting effects of the policy-borrowing process (Watson, 2001). The latter has enhanced its contentious and complex nature and it is no coincidence that inclusion is characterized by multiplicity of meanings (Graham and Slee, 2008b), as well as varied and diverse 'manifestations in practice' (Lindsay, 2003: 1). The metaphor of inclusion as a travelling theory that is 'tamed' and 'domesticated' across time and space (Said, 2000; cited in Slee, 2006: 113) can be extended to include the ways in which the notion of inclusion is also 'hybridized' by becoming entwined with, and imbued by, a host of contextual social and cultural dynamics.

As already discussed, globalization is by no means expected to undermine the role of cross-cultural research. Rather it will spawn fresh perspectives to engage with, and necessitate the utilization of different methodological approaches (Dale, 2000) capable, among other things, of identifying what Ochs and Phillips (2004) call the 'filters' that are at work in the policy-borrowing process. As Dale (1999: 4–5) puts it: 'Globalization may change the parameters and direction of state policies in similar ways but it does not inevitably override or remove existing national peculiarities (or different sectoral peculiarities within national societies).' Hence, it is crucially important to engage with the dialectic of the global, the national and the local (Crossley and Watson, 2003).

The notion of 'glocalization' (Robertson, 1995; cited in Green, 2002) epitomizes the dialectic of the global and the local in the policy-borrowing process, whereby local cultures, language and ideological dynamics infiltrate and eventually domesticate inclusive educational policies. Postmodern theoretical frameworks affirm the importance of adopting a multidimensional and cross-cultural approach to understanding and critiquing social reality whereby

> politics . . . takes on new forms and content . . . as culture plays a more crucial role in domains from the economy to personal identity, and as capital creates a new global economy and new syntheses of the global and the local abound. (Best and Kellner, 2001: 104)

Inclusive education policymaking in many parts of the world mirror the abusive dimension of the policy-borrowing process (Watson, 2001; Liasidou, 2008). Levin (1998), for instance, refers to this process as an international trend, and characterizes it as 'epidemic of education policy', inasmuch as policies are spread either in haphazard and uncontrolled ways or through coordinated networks of dissemination.

In the pursuit of educational innovations and reforms in alignment with the demands of global economy, policymakers across the globe look to the West for education policy 'quick fixes' and modernization initiatives through the process of policy borrowing. Inclusion has proved to be very high in the educational reform agendas, which are characterized by 'false universalism' (Nguyen et al., 2009: 109); whereby inclusive education policies have been uncritically introduced and implemented, without taking into consideration the contextual dynamics impacting on the policymaking process. This reflects what Noah (1984; cited in Watson, 2001: 12) calls the 'use and abuse of comparative research', implying the illusive and erroneous expectancy that what works in a country can be introduced and implemented in another socio-historical context.

The Education for All (EFA) movement constitutes a manifestation of a globalizing discourse of inclusion, promoted in different forms across different geopolitical jurisdictions. The globalizing discourse of inclusion has been, however, characterized as a new form of cultural imperialism, whereby educational policy initiatives in countries of the North are uncritically transferred to countries of the South (South refers to lesser developed countries) without taking into consideration their idiomorphic socio-historical characteristics. Grench (2011) analyses the ways in which knowledge and practices from the North are indiscriminately transferred to the countries of the South ignoring the ways in which disability is understood, negotiated and experienced in contexts of the majority world (countries of the South).

Cultural imperialism, evidenced in the negative dimension of educational policy-borrowing process and the spiral of economic dependency of the countries of the South, has been characterized as a form of neo-colonialism, whereby relations of subordination and colonial control are sustained and perpetuated, albeit in subtle ways. Education constitutes 'a significant instrument of neo-colonial influence' (Bray, 1993: 334) manifested through 'educational neo-colonialism' (Nguyen et al., 2009: 109), whereby West-centric educational imperatives influence educational systems internationally through the process of globalization. As Alur (2007: 98) points out, 'colonialism may officially have come to an end . . . but a new era of colonialism has taken over . . . by Western experts.'

Neo-liberal globalizing discourses disseminated by supranational organizations influence the ways in which disability is experienced and affected in the developing countries of the South. For instance, neo-liberal imperatives view disabled people as part of the poverty problem faced by developing countries of the South, because disabled people are not expected to contribute to market-oriented and profit-maximizing activities. The spiral of economic dependency of these countries on international donors (e.g., World Bank) necessitates high performance indicators and immediate results, and neither of these aspirations are expected to be fulfilled by disabled people. As a result, disabled people are regarded as being an 'unattractive proposal' (Grench, 2011: 96) because they require resources and ongoing commitment, an investment that cannot yield immediate results (especially in terms of providing inclusive education for disabled individuals).

Moreover, neo-liberal globalizing discourses necessitate development initiatives informed by profit-maximizing and efficiency criteria, which can potentially contribute to disablement. These initiatives, are concerned with 'exploring alternatives to direct public provision' whereby 'corporatisation and privatisation are important policy options in this context' (OECD, 1995: 9; cited in Ball, 2009: 44) The privatisation of water in countries of the South, for instance, despite maximizing profit for foreign companies, prevents the poorest from having access, and subsequently, maximizes the risk of impairments such as river blindness and other related diseases. This is a significant aspect of the globalizing discourse of inclusion and raises certain questions as to the ways in which the rhetoric around 'inclusion' and 'rights' promulgated in countries of the North can be applied in majority world countries, where people have unmet basic needs upon which depends their survival. This is especially true when we bear in mind that almost half of the population in these countries acquire diseases due to lack of clean water (Grench, 2011).

The rhetoric of inclusion and disability necessitates a global discussion on disability and inclusive education that does not homogenize and silence the peculiarities of diverse socio-political contexts, especially in countries of the South. Understandings of, and responses to, inclusion and disability should be contextually grounded taking into consideration the specificities of diverse histories of local, regional and national contexts. As Miles (2007: 5.3) writes with regard to the necessity to develop international strategies for disability-related work in developing countries:

> Meaningful 'inclusion' is hardly a realistic proposition in the typical hugely crowded classrooms where isolated teachers with little support, no equipment and tiny (often unpaid), salary struggle to give a smattering of education to half the world's children, many of whom have unnoticed impairments, chronic illnesses and disabling nutritional deficiencies.

Reflective Exercises

To what extent and under what conditions can Western-centric inclusive education policies and practices become global?

In what ways are aspects of neo-colonialism reflecting the interests of global capitalism, influence the ways in which disability is viewed and experienced in developing countries?

Useful Websites

UNESCO international Bureau of Education
    www.ibe.unesco.org/en.html
Eurydice-Network on education systems and policies in Europe
    eacea.ec.europa.eu/education/eurydice/index_en.php
Advancing Educational Inclusion and Quality in South East Europe
    www.see-educoop.net/aeiq/index.htm
Inclusion Interamericana
    www.inclusion-ia.org/indexeng.htm
Inclusion International
    www.inclusion-international.org/

8

Conclusions

Inclusion has taken many configurations, has been variously interpreted, understood, conceptualized, theorized and yet, it remains a largely vague, contested, and debated notion, which can be either enthusiastically proclaimed or blatantly denounced. The latter stance is not surprising, given that inclusion envisages an emancipatory educational and social transformation, which, admittedly, is a rather demanding and thorny pursuit. This is because inclusion is contingent on, and intertwined with, a vast array of vexed and complex issues that need to be destabilized and repositioned in the pursuit of transformative change. In effect, inclusion has become an all-encompassing term whose understanding necessitates exploring a constellation of conceptual and pragmatic dynamics that constitute its essentially multidimensional nature.

The book has been concerned with providing an alternative way of conceiving and understanding the complexities of inclusive education policymaking. This has involved challenging unidimensional and deficit views of disabled students, and identifying and exploring the interplay of power relations embodied in the matrices of biographical, political, ideological, social and cultural factors that constitute barriers to change. This has required the employment of a cross-disciplinary and critical framework of social analysis in order to document and exemplify the 'polymorphous interweaving of correlations' (Foucault, 1991: 58) implicated in the process of inclusive education policymaking, with a view to critiquing and destabilizing the special education status quo. Attention has focused on identifying and exploring the dominant frame of reference within which the various discourses underpinning inclusive education policymaking emerge and get reified, through institutional arrangements and attitudinal regimes. Moreover, this has involved raising questions and providing a critical analysis of the ideologies, discourses and related practices within the field. The struggles for greater inclusive policies and practices have been exemplified against a complicated network whereby power and knowledge become indispensable and engender the dominant discourses underpinning the processes and outcomes of inclusive education policymaking.

The process of change necessitates a realistic understanding of the profundity of issues embroiled in the social and political struggles for inclusion without, however, subscribing to theoretical pessimism and political inertia. The oppressive and subjugating dimensions of the power/knowledge couplet do not negate the productive effects of power and the feasibility of transformative change. Foucault is not only concerned with power, but also with the existence of different loci of resistance. Even though he does not negate the existence of centralized loci of power (e.g., the State/official legislation), he acknowledges the pervasive influence of a decentralized body of heterogeneous power relations that are played out and acted upon across society (Foucault, 1979b; 1980a). 'Bottom up' and decentralized conceptualizations of power open up liberating opportunities for resistance by means of localized struggles As he succinctly puts it: 'Where there is power, there is resistance and yet, or rather consequently, this resistance is never in a position of exteriority in relation to power' (Foucault, 1990: 95).

'Resistance' can be conceptualized as being a 'source of celebration' (Kendall and Wickham, 1999: 51) and can only be mobilized when there is a clear and consistent moral vision articulated in unambiguous legislative mandates and political initiatives. Shapiro (1989: 36), while writing about educational change, gives considerable prominence to: 'the critical necessity of a clearly enunciated moral vision to an effective politics of educational change'. It is necessary, however, that this vision should jointly permeate the 'context of influence', the 'context of policy text production' and the 'context of practice' (Ball and Bowe, 1992).

Crucially, an important aspect of resistance should be oriented to the language we use and the metaphors we deploy to describe disabled people, their education and their life. The power of language and its discursive embodiments constitute an immense, albeit an opaque, impediment that, unless deconstructed, will continue to undermine any attempts towards inclusion. The critical examination of language, ideology and discourse open up new analytical avenues and conceptual frameworks in order to understand 'the constitution of not just human subjectivity and social relations, but also social control and surveillance, the governance of polity and nation-state, and attendant modes of domination and marginalisation' (Luke, 2002: 99).

The critical dimension of the struggles towards greater inclusive policy and practice entail re-authoring and valorizing the notion of disability and creating a 'new disability discourse' (Corker, 1999: 192). To this end, it is imperative to devise a new language of disability through which negative implications are subverted and reconfigured. Insofar as the language of special needs remains intact, little can be done in order to challenge negative connotations associated with disability.

Notwithstanding ample rhetoric in safeguarding and reinstating their rights, disabled people are still to a significant extent discriminated against in terms of their human attributes, in much the same way as people might be still widely discriminated on the basis of their colour, ethnicity or gender. Exclusion still affects great masses of people and it should be constantly included in the debate agenda favouring social and educational change. However, the distinctiveness of exclusion in terms of disability lies in the fact that far from being reduced as it might have happened with colour or gender, it has been steadfastly becoming a sophisticated process that can occasionally be very difficult to be uncovered and tackled (Slee, 1996a, 2001a,b,c).

Struggles over greater inclusion are ongoing, and entail questioning policies and practices, not only in terms of inclusion but also in terms of its constituent issues such as human rights, citizenship education, social justice and equality of opportunity. This can only be achieved when we instigate a paradigm shift from a reductionist epistemology to an interdisciplinary analytical platform intended to expose the historicized and contextualized dimensions of disability and special educational needs. By no means can the institutionalized and culturally ingrained 'regimes of truth' (Foucault, 1984a) undermining the attempts towards inclusion be challenged, unless there is the ideological platform and institutional infrastructure needed towards this direction. Otherwise, these 'regimes of truth' will be further consolidated and naturalized thereby corroborating and perpetuating the historical imperatives of special education thinking. The contradictory discursive reality and 'ideological impurity' (Norwich, 1996; 2010) underpinning special and inclusive educational policymaking need to be critically examined against the interplay of agency and structure in the attempts for transformative change. The latter entails recognizing, as Graham and Slee (2008: 85) write, the 'conjoined nature of inclusion and exclusion . . . and interrogat(ing) the normative assumptions that lead us to think we can even talk of "including"'.

The debate on inclusion is ongoing and will presumably never end; the crucial point, therefore, is to be willing and be well aware of the necessity to be constantly and seriously engaged in the critical process of further analysis and research in exploring 'innovative possibilities' (Best and Kellner,

2001: 102) for transformative change. Towards this end, the struggles must assume neither complacency (Barton, 2005) nor abdication resulting from either chimerical or nihilistic arbitrations over the feasibility of inclusion. Inclusion is neither a utopian nor an uncontested pursuit. It is a demanding and slow process that necessitates commitment, vision and action, as well as an informed recognition of the perennial character of the struggles for transformative change. Having acknowledged that the existence of achievable 'ends' is an infeasible pursuit, inclusion should be regarded as a process of '*becoming*' rather than 'being'.

Given the complexity and the challenges that the issues under consideration have presented, this book is very much an 'unfinished and necessarily imperfect' (Said, 1994: 17; cited in Ball, 2006: 5) theoretical venture and, thus, offers a partial and incomplete account. It has been, nevertheless, an attempt to develop critical and reflexive understanding particularly relating to grappling with the assemblage of ideas involved in the engagement of multiple perspectives underpinning inclusive education policy and practice.

Reflective Exercise

Why is it necessary to maintain continuous and critical debate about inclusion?

Bibliography

Agger, B. (1991). 'Critical theory, poststructuralism, postmodernism: There sociological relevance'. *Annual Review of Sociology*, 17, 105–31.

Ainscow, M. (2005a). 'Developing inclusive education systems: What are the levers for change?' *Journal of Educational Change,* 6(2), 109–24.

— (2005b). 'The next big challenge: Inclusive school improvement'. Keynote presentation at the Conference of School Effectiveness and Improvement, Barcelona, January, 2005.

— (2000). 'The next step for special education: Supporting the development of inclusive practices'. *British Journal of Special Education*, 27(2), 76–80.

— (1998). 'Developing links between special needs and school improvement'. *Support for Learning*, 13(2), 70–75.

— (1997). 'Towards inclusive schooling'. *British Journal of Special Education*, 24(1), 3–6.

Ainscow, M., Booth, A., Dyson, P., Farrell, J., Frankham, F., Gallannaugh A., Howes and R. Smith. (2006). *Improving Schools, Developing Inclusion*. London: Routledge.

Ainscow, M. and Cesar, M. (2006). 'Inclusive education ten years after the Salamanca: Setting the agenda'. *European Journal of Psychology of Education*, xxi, 3, 231–38.

Ainscow, M. and Miles, S. (2008). 'Making education for all inclusive: Where next?' *Prospects*, 38, 15–34.

Alexander, R. (2009). 'The Cambridge Primary Review and Its Final Report.' *Royal Society of Arts*, 19 October 2009. Available online at www.thersa.org/__data/assets/pdf_file/0004/248026/RSA-091019.pdf.

Allan, J. (2005). 'Inclusion as an ethical project'. In Tremain, S. (ed.), *Foucault and the Government of Disability*, pp. 281–298. Michigan, IL: University of Michigan Press.

— (2004). 'Deterritorializations: Putting postmodernism to work on teacher education and inclusion'. *Educational Philosophy and Theory*, 36(4), 417–32.

Allen, B. (2005). 'Foucault's nominalism'. In Tremain, S. (ed.), *Foucault and the Government of Disability*. Michigan: The University of Michigan Press.

Althusser, L. (1994). 'Ideology and ideological state apparatuses (notes towards an investigation). In S. Zizek (ed.), *Mapping Ideology*. New York: Verso.

Alur, M. (2007). 'The lethargy of a nation: Inclusive education in India'. In Barton, L. and Armstrong, F. (eds), *Policy, Experience and Change: Cross–Cultural Reflections on Inclusive Education*, pp. 91–106. Dordrecht, The Netherlands: Springer.

Anderson, G. (1990). 'Towards a critical constructivist approach to school administration: Invisibility, legitimation and the study of non-events'. *Education Administration Quarterly*, 26(1), 38–59.

Angelides, P. (2004). 'Moving towards inclusive education in Cyprus?' *International Journal of Inclusive Education,* 8(4), 407–22.

Apple, M. (2000). *Official Knowledge: Democratic Education in a Conservative Age.* Great Britain: Routledge.

Archer, M. (1982). 'Morphogenesis versus structuration: On combining structure and action'. *The British Journal of Sociology,* 33(4), 455–83.

Armstrong, D. (2005). 'Reinventing 'inclusion': New Labour and the cultural politics of special education'. *Oxford Review of Education,* 31(1), 135–51.

— (2003). *Spaced Out: Policy, Difference and the Challenge of Inclusive Education.* London: Kluwer Academic Publishers.

— (2002). 'Managing difference: inclusion, performance and power'. *Critical Quarterly,* 44(4), 51–6.

— (1999). 'Histories of inclusion: Perspectives on the history of special education'. In Barton, L. and Armstrong, F. (eds), *Difference and Difficulty: Insights, Issues and Dilemmas.* Sheffiield: University of Sheffield.

— (1995). *Power and Partnership in Education.* London: Routledge.

Armstrong, F., Belmont, B. and Verillon, A. (2000). '"Vive la difference" exploring content, context, policy and change in special education in France: Developing cross–cultural collaboration'. In Armstrong, F., Armstrong, D. and Barton L. (eds), *Inclusive Education. Policy, Contexts and Comparative Perspectives.* London: David Fulton.

Armstrong, A. C., Armstrong, D. and Spandagou. (2010). *Inclusive Education: International Policy and Practice.* London: Sage.

Armstrong, Th. (2009). *Multiple Intelligences in the Classroom.* Alexandria: ASCD.

Arnove, R. (2003). 'Introduction: Reframing comparative education. The dialectic of the global and the local'. In Arnove R. and Torres C. A. (eds), *Comparative Education. The Dialectic of the Global and the Local.* USA: Rowman and Littlefield.

Artiles, A. J. (1998). 'The dilemma of difference: Enriching the disproportionality discourse with theory and context'. *Journal of Special Education,* 32(1), 32–6.

Artiles, A. J., Harris–Murri, N. and Rostenberg, D. (2006). 'Inclusion as social justice: Critical notes on discourses, assumptions, and the road ahead'. *Theory into Practice,* 45(3), 260–8.

Atkinson, P. A. and Coffey, A. (1997). 'Analysing documentary realities'. In Silverman, D. (ed.), *Qualitative Research,* pp. 45–62. *Theory, Methods and Practice.* London: Sage.

Avramidis, E. and Norwich, B. (2002). 'Teachers' attitudes towards integration/inclusion: A review of the literature'. *European Journal of Special Needs Education,* 17(2), 129–47.

Bacchi (2000). 'Policy as discourse: What does it mean? Where does it get us?' *Discourse,* 21(1), 45–57.

Baert, P. (1998). *Social Theory in the Twentieth Century.* Cambridge: Polity.

Baker, B. and Heyning, K. (eds). (2004). *Dangerous Coagulations? The Uses of Foucault in the Study of Education.* Peter Lang: New York.

Ball, S. (2009). *The Education Debate.* Bristol: Policy Press.

— (2008). 'The legacy of ERA, privatization and the policy ratchet'. *Educational Management Administration and Leadership,* 36(2), 185–99.

— (2007). *Education plc: Understanding Private Sector Participation in Public Sector Education*. London: Routledge.

— (2004a). 'Performativities and fabrications in the education economy: Towards a perfomative society'. In Ball, S. (ed.), *The RoutledgeFalmer Reader in the Sociology of Education*. London: Routledge Falmer, 143–55.

— (2004b). 'Education for sale! The commodification of everything?' King's Annual Education Lecture, 2004, University of London, 17 June 2004. Available online at http://nepc.colorado.edu/files/CERU–0410–253–OWI.pdf.

— (2003). 'The teacher's soul and the terrors of Performativity'. *Journal of Education Policy*, 18(2), 215–18.

— (1999). 'Labour, learning and the economy: A "policy sociology" perspective'. *Cambridge Journal of Education*, 29(2), 195–206.

— (1998a). 'Big Policies/Small World: An introduction to international perspectives in education policy'. *Comparative Education*, 34(2), 119–30.

— (1998b). 'Ethics, self–interest and the market form in education'. In Cribb, A. (ed.), *Markets, Managers and Public Service? Professional Ethics in the New Welfare State*, Centre for Public Policy Research, Occasional Paper, No. 1. London: Kings College.

— (1997). 'Policy sociology and critical social research: A personal review of recent education policy and policy research'. *British Educational Research Journal*, 23(3), 257–73.

— (1994a). 'Some Reflections on policy theory; a brief response to Hateher and Troyna'. *Journal of Education Policy*, 9(2), 171–82.

— (1994b). *Education Reform. a Critical and Post–Structural Approach*. Buckingham: Open University Press.

— (1994c). 'Researching inside the state: Issues in the interpretation of elite interviews'. In Halpin, D. and Troyna, B. (eds), *Researching Education Policy. Ethical and Methodological Issues*. London: The Falmer Press.

— (1993). 'What is policy? Texts, trajectories and toolboxes'. *Discourse*, 13(2), 10–17.

— (1990). *Politics and Policymaking in Education*. London: Routledge.

Ball, S. J. (2006). 'The Necessity and Violence of Theory'. *Discourse*, 27(1), 3–10.

Ball, S. and Bowe, R. (1992). 'Subject departments and the "implementation" of national curriculum policy: An overview of the issues'. *Journal of Curriculum Studies*, 24(2), 97–115.

Ballard, K. (2004). 'Ideology and the origins of exclusion: A case study'. In Ware, L. (ed.), *Ideology and the Politics of (In) Exclusion*, pp. 89–107. Peter Lang: New York.

Barbules, N. C. (1992). 'Forms of ideology–critique: A pedagogical perspective'. *International Journal of Qualitative Studies in Education*, 5(1), 7–17.

Barnes, C. (1996). 'Theories of disability and the origins of oppression of disabled people in Western society'. In Barton, L., (ed.), *Disability and Society: Emerging Issues and Insights*. London: Longman.

Barnes, C., Mercer, G. and Shakespear, T. (1999). *Exploring Disability*. Cambridge: Polity Press.

Barnes, C. and Mercer, G. (2005). *Disability*. Cambridge: Polity Press.

Barton, L. (2008a). 'Foreword'. In Gabel, S. and Danforth, S. (eds), *Disability and the Politics of Education*. NewYork: Peter Lang.

— (2008b). 'Inclusive education, teachers and the politics of possibility'. Paper presented at The Inclusion Festival, 21 January, Utrecht, Holland.

— (2005). 'Emancipatory research and disabled people: Some observations and questions'. *Educational Review,* 57(3), 317–27.

— (2003). 'Inclusive education and teacher education: A basis for hope or a discourse of delusion?' Professorial Lecture. Institute of Education, University of London.

— (1999a). 'Market ideologies, education and the challenge for inclusion'. In Mitchell, D., (ed.), (2004) *Special Educational Needs and Inclusive Education. 1. Major Themes in Education. Systems and Contexts.* London: Routledge; Falmer.

— (1999b). 'The politics of special education needs'. In Oliver, M. and Barton, L. (eds), *Disability Studies Today: Past, Present and Future.* Leeds: The Disability Press.

— (1997). 'Inclusive education: Romantic, subversive or realistic?' In *International Journal of Inclusive Education,* 1(3), 231–42.

— (1996). 'Politics, marketisation and the struggle for inclusive education'. *Hitsubashi Journal of Social Studies,* 28, 29–43.

— (1995). 'The politics of education for all'. *Support for Learning,* 10(4), 156–61.

— (1993). 'The struggle for citizenship: The case of disabled people'. *Disability, Handicap and Society,* 8(3), 235–46.

— (1988a). *The Politics of Special Education.* London: The Falmer Press.

— (1988b). 'Research practice: The need for alternative perspective'. In Barton, L. (ed.), *The Politics of Special Education Needs: An Introduction,* pp. 79–94. London: Falmer.

— (1986). 'The politics of special educational needs'. *Disability, Handicap and Society,* 1(3), 273–90.

Barton, L. and Armstrong, F. (2001). 'Disability, education, and inclusion: Cross–cultural issues and dilemmas'. In Albrecht, G., Seelman, K. and Bury, M. (eds), *The Handbook of Disability Studies.* London: Sage.

— (2007). *Policy, Experience and Change: Cross–Cultural Reflections on Inclusive Education.* Dordrecht: Springer.

Barton, L. and Oliver, M. (1992). 'Special needs: Personal troubles or public issues?' In Arnot, M. and Barton, L. (eds), *Voicing Concerns: Sociological Perspectives on Contemporary Education Reform,* Wallingford, UK: Triangle Books.

Barton, L. and Slee, R. (1999). 'Competition, selection and inclusive education: some observations'. *International Journal of Inclusive Education,* 3(1), 3–12.

Barton, L. and Tomlinson, S. (eds) (1984). *Special Education and Social Interests.* UK: Croom Helm LMD.

Baxter, J. (2003). *Positioning Gender in Discourse: A Feminist Methodology.* Basingstoke: Palgrave Macmillan.

Beck, J. (1999). 'Makeover or takeover?The strange death of educational autonomy in neo–liberal England'. *British Journal of Sociology of Education,* 20(2), 223–38.

Beck, J. (2009). 'Appropriating professionalism: Restructuring the official knowledge base of England's "modernised" teaching profession'. *British Journal of Sociology of Education,* 3(1), 3–14.

Belanger, N. (2001). 'Solicitude and special education policies'. *Cambridge Journal of Education,* 31(5), 337–47.

Benjamin, S. (2002a). 'Valuing diversity: a cliché for the 21st century?' *International Journal of Inclusive Education*, 6(4), 309–23.

— (2002b). *The Micropolitics of Inclusive Education*. Buckingham: Open University Press.

Benton, T. and Craib, I. (2001). *Philosophy of Social Science: The Philosophical Foundations of Social Thought*. Basingstoke: Palgrave.

Best, S. and Kellner, D. (2001). 'Dawns, twilights, and transitions: postmodern theories, politics and challenges'. *Democracy and Nature*, 7(1), 101–17.

Billing, M. (1991). *Ideology and Opinions: Studies in Rhetorical Psychology*. London: Sage.

Blades, D. (1997). *Procedures of Power and Curriculum Change: Foucault and the Quest for Possibilities in Science Education*. New York: Peter Lang.

Blommaert, J. (2005). *Discourse: Key Topics in Sociolinguistics*. UK: Cambridge University Press.

Booth, T. (2003). 'Vewing inclusion from a distance: Gaining perspective from a comparative study'. In Nind, M., Rix, J., Sheehy, K., and Simmons, K. (eds), *Inclusive Education: Diverse Perspectives*. UK: David Fulton.

Booth, T. and Ainscow, M. (2002). *The Index for Inclusion* (2nd edn) Bristol: Centre for Studies in Inclusive Education.

Bottery, M. (2000*). Education, Policy and Ethics*. London: Continuum.

Boyd, W. L. (1992). 'The power of paradigms: Reconceptualising educational policy and management'. *Educational Administration Quarterly*, 28(4), 504–28.

Bowe, R., Ball, S. and Gold, A. (1992). *Reforming Education and Changing Schools: Case Studies in Policy Sociology*. London: Routledge.

Brantlinger, E. (2004). 'Ideologies discerned, values determined: Getting past the hierarchies of special education'. In Ware, L. (ed.), *Ideology and the Politics of (In) Exclusion*, pp. 11–31. Peter Lang: New York.

— (1997). 'Using ideology: Cases of nonrecognition of the politics of research and practice in special education'. *Review of Educational Research*, 67(4), 425–59.

Bray, M. (1993). 'Education and the vestiges of colonialism: Self-dermination, neo-colonialism and dependency in the South Pacific'. *Comparative Education*, 29(3), 333–48.

Brehony, K. (2005). 'Primary schooling under New Labour: The irresolvable contradiction of excellence and enjoyment'. *Oxford Review of Education*, 31(1), 29–46.

Burgstahler, S. and Cory, R. (2008). 'Moving in from the margins: From accommodation to universal design'. In Gabel, S. and Danforth, S. (eds), *Disability and the Politics of Education*. New York: Peter Lang.

Burk, P. J. and Ruedel, K. (2008). 'Disability classification, categorization in education'. In Florian, L. and McLaughlin, M. (eds), *Disability Classification in Education*. London: Sage.

Bury, M. (2000). 'On chronic illness and disability'. In Bird, C. E., Conrad, P. and Fremont, A. M. (eds), *Handbook of Medical Sociology* (5th edn). New Jersey, PA: Prentice Hall.

Campbell, F. K. (2005). 'Legislating disability: Negative ontologies and the government of legal identities'. In Tremain, S. (ed.), *Foucault and the Government of Disability*, pp. 108–132. Michigan, IL: University of Michigan Press.

Carlson, L. (2005). 'Docile bodies, docile minds: Foucauldian reflections on mental retardation'. In Tremain, S. (ed.), *Foucault and the Government of Disability*, pp. 133–152. Michigan, IL: University of Michigan Press.

Christensen, C. (1996). 'Disabled, handicapped or disordered: "What's in a name?" In Christensen, C. and Rizvi, F. (eds), *Disability and the Dilemmas of Education and Justice*, pp. 63–78. Great Britain: Open University Press.

Cigman, R. (2006). *Included or Excluded?* London: Routledge.

Claxton, G. and Carr, M. (2004). 'A framework for teaching learning: the dynamics of disposition'. *Early Years*, 24(1), 87–97.

Clough, P. and Corbett, J. (eds) (2000). *Theories of Inclusive Education. A Students Guide.* London: Routledge.

Codd, J. (1988). 'The construction and deconstruction of educational policy documents'. *Journal of Education Policy*, 3(3), 235–47.

Cohen, I. (1989). *Structuration Theory: Anthony Giddens and the Constitution of Social Life.* London: MacMullan Education Ltd.

Cole, B. (2005). 'Mission impossible? Special educational needs, inclusion and the re–conceptualization of the role of the SENCO in England and Wales'. *European Journal of Special Meds Education*, 20(3), 287–307.

Cornwall, J. (1997). *Access to Learning for Pupils with Disabilities.* London: David Fulton.

Corbett, J. (1996). *Bad–Mouthing: The Language of Special Needs.* London: The Falmer Press.

— (1993). 'Postmodernism and the "Special Needs" metaphors'. *Oxford Review of Education*, 19(4), 547–53.

Corbett, J. and Norwich, B. (1998). 'The contribution of special education to our understanding of values, schooling and the curriculum'. *Pedagogy, Culture & Society*, 6(1), 85–96.

Corker, M. (1999). 'New disability discourse, the principle of optimisation and social change'. In Corker, M. and French, S. (eds), *Disability Discourse*, 192–210. Buckingham: Open University Press.

Corker, M. and Shakespeare, T. (eds) (2002a). *Disability/Postmodernity*, pp. 1–17. London: Continuum.

— (2002b). 'Mapping the terrain'. In *Disability/Postmodernity*, London: Continuum.

Corker, M. and French, S. (1999). 'Reclaiming discourse in disability studies'. In Corker, M. and French, S. (eds), *Disability Discourse*, pp. 1–11. Buckingham: Open University Press.

Cranston, N., Ehrich, L., Kimber, M. (2005). 'Ethical dilemmas: The "bread and butter" of educational leaders' lives'. *Journal of Educational Administration*, 44(2), 106–21.

Croll, P. and Moses, D. (1994). 'Policy–making and special educational needs: A framework for analysis', *European Journal of Special Needs Education*, 9(3), 275–86.

— (1989). 'Policy and practice in special education: The implementation of the 1981 Education Act in England and Wales'. In Brown, R. and Chazan, M. (eds), *Learning Difficulties and Emotional Problems,* 23–38 Calgary, Alberta: Detselig.

Crossley, M. and Watson, K. (2003). *Comparative and International Research in Education: Globalisation, Context and Difference.* London: Routledge Falmer.

Crotty, M. (1998). *The Foundations of Social Research: Meaning and Perspective in Research Process.* London: Sage.

Crow, L. (1996). 'Including all our lives: Renewing the social model of disability'. In Barnes, C. and Mercer, G. (eds), *Exploring the Divide: Illness and Disability.* Leeds: The Disability Press.

Dale, R. (2000). 'Globalization: A new world for comparative education?' In Schriewer, J. (ed.), *Discourse Formation in Comparative Education*, pp. 87–110. Oxford: Peter Lang.

— (1999). 'Specifying globalization effects on national policy: A focus on the mechanisms'. *Journal of Education Policy*, 14(1), 1–17.

Dale, R. and Ozga, J. (1993). 'Two hemispheres – Both "New Right"?: 1980's education reform in New Zealand and England and Wales'. In Lingard, B, Knight, J. and Porter, P. (eds), *Schooling Reform in Hard Times*, pp. 63–87. London: The Falmer Press.

Danforth, S. and Rhodes, W. C. (1997). 'Deconstructing disability', *Remedial and Special Education*, 18(6), 357–67.

Danzinger, M. (1995). 'Policy analysis postmodernized: Some political and pedagogical ramifications'. *Policy Studies Journal*, 23(3), 435–50.

David, J. and Greene, D. (1983). 'Organizational barriers to full implementation of PL'. In Chambers, J. and Hartman, W. (eds), *Special Education Policies: Their History, Implementation and Finance*, pp. 94–142. Philadelphia: Temple University Press.

Davies, E. A. and Miyake, N. (2004). 'Explorations of scaffolding in complex classroom systems'. *Journal of the Learning Sciences*, 13(3), 265–72.

Davis, P. and Florian, L. (2004). 'Teaching strategies and approaches for pupils with Special Educational Needs: A scoping study'. Brief No RB516 (London: DfES). Available online at: www.dfes.gov.uk/research/data/uploadfiles/RB516.doc (Accessed 18 November 2010).

Day, C. (2005). 'Sustaining success in challenging contexts: Leadership in English schools'. *Journal of Educational Administration*, 43(6), 573–83.

DCSF (Department for Children, Schools and Families) (2009a). 'Breaking the link between disadvantage and low attainment – Everyone's business.' Annesley: DCSF.

— (2009b). 'Your child, your schools, our future: Building a 21st century schools system'. Annesley: DCSF.

— (2009c). 'Independent review of the primary curriculum: Final report'. Annesley: DCSF.

— (2009d). 'Lamb inquiry – special educational needs and parental confidence'. Annesley: DCSF.

— (2007). 'Social and emotional aspects of learning'. Annesley: DCSF.

Dean, M. (2010). *Governmentality: Power and Rule in Modern Society*. London Sage.

DfE (Department for Education) (2011a). 'Leading on intervention: Strengthening the quality of everyday inclusive teaching'. The waves of intervention model. Available online at: http://nationalstrategies.standards.dcsf.gov.uk/node/41795 (Accessed 16 june 2011).

— (2011b). *Support and Aspiration: A New Approach to Special Educational Needs and Disability*. UK: TSO.

DfES (Department for Education and Skills) (2006). 'The common assessment framework for children and young people: Practitioners' guide'. Annesley, UK: DfES.

— (2004). 'Removing barriers to achievement: The Government's strategy for SEN'. London: DfES.

— (2003a). 'Excellence and enjoyment: A strategy for primary schools'. London, DfES.

— (2003b). 'Every child matters: Green paper on children's services'. Norwich: The Stationery Office.

— (2001). 'Special educational needs code of practice'. Nottingham: DfES.

Derrida, J. (1979). *Positions*. Chicago: University of Chicago Press.

— (1976). *Of Grammatology*. Baltimore: Johns Hopkins University Press.

Drake, R. (1999). *Understanding Disability Policies*. London: McMillan Press LTD.

Dreyfus, H. and Rabinow, P. (1982). *Michel Foucault. Beyond Structuralism and Hermeneytics*. Great Britain: The Harvest Press Limited.

Duncan, N. (2003). 'Awkward customers?: Parents and provision for special educational needs'. *Disability & Society*, 18(3), 341–56.

Dyson, A. (2005). 'Philosophy, politics and economics?: The story of inclusive education in England'. In Mitchell. D., *Contextualising Inclusive Education: Evaluating Old and New International Perspectives*, pp. 63–88. London: Routledge.

— (2001). 'Special needs in the twenty–first century: Where we've been and where we're going'. *British Journal of Special Education*, 28(1), 24–9.

— (1999). 'Inclusion and inclusions: theories and discourses in inclusive education'. In Daniels, H. and Garner, P. (eds), *World Yearbook of Education 1999: Inclusive Education*, pp. 36–53. London: Kogan Page.

Dyson, D. and Howes, A. J. (2009). 'Towards an interdisciplinary research agenda for inclusive education'. In Hick, P., Kershner, R. and P. Farrell (eds), *Psychology for Inclusive Education*, London: Routledge.

Eagleton, T. (1991). *Ideology*. UK: Verson.

Ekins and Grimes (2009). *Inclusion: Developing an Effective Whole School Approach*. England: Open University Press.

Ellis, S., Tod, J. and Matheson–Graham, L. (2008). *Special Educational Needs and Inclusion*. UK: NASUWT.

Elwan, A. (1999). *Poverty and disability: A survey of literature. Social protection*. Unit Human Development Network The World Bank. Available online at http://siteresources.worldbank.org/DISABILITY/Resources/2806581172608138489/PovertyDisabElwan.pdf (Accessed 19 May 2011).

Evans, J. (2007). 'Forms of provision and models of service delivery'. In Florian, L. (ed.), *The SAGE Handbook of Special Education*. London: Sage.

— (1994). 'Whatever happened to the subject and the state in policy research in education?' *Discourse*, 14(2), 57–64.

Farrell, M. (2009). *Foundations of Special Education*. UK: Blackwell.

Fairclough, N. (2001). *Language and Power*. UK: Longman.

— (2000). 'Discourse, social theory and social research: The discourse of welfare reform'. *Journal of Sociolinguistics*, 4(2), 163–95.

— (1999). *Critical Discourse Analysis: The Critical Study of Language*. London: Longman.

— (1993). *Discourse and Social Change*. Cambridge: Polity Press.

Feiler, A. and Gibson, H. (1999). 'Threats to the inclusive movement'. *British Journal of Special Education*, 26(3), 147–152.

Fitch, F (2003). 'Inclusion, exclusion and ideology: Special education students' changing sense of self.' *The Urban Review*, 35(3), 233–52.

Fletcher-Cambell, F. (2002). The financing of special education: lessons from Europe. *Support for Learning*, 17(1), 19–22.

Florian, L., Rose, R. and Tilstone, C. (eds) (1998). *Planning Inclusive Practice*. London: Routledge.

Foucault, M. (1991). 'Politics and the study of discourse'. In Butchel, G., Gordon, C. and Miller, P. (eds), *The Foucault Effect: Studies in Governmentality*, pp. 53–72. USA: The University of Chicago Press.

— (1990). *The History of Sexuality, Vol. 1. An Introduction.* New York: Vintage.

— (1988). 'Power and sex'. In L. D. Kritzman (ed.), *Michel Foucault: Politics, Philosophy, Culture,* 110–14. New York: Routledge.

— (1984a). 'The order of discourse'. In Shapiro, M. (ed.) *Language and Politics*. Great Britain: Blackwell.

— (1984b). 'Nietzsche, genealogy, history'. In Rabinow, P. (ed.), *The Foucault Reader*. Harmondsworth: Penguin Books.

— (1980a). 'Truth and Power'. In Gordon, C. (ed.) *Power/knowledge; Selected Interviews and Other Writings,* 1972–1977. Brighton: Harvester Press.

— (1980b). 'Discourse, Power and Knowledge'. In Sheridan, A. (ed.) *The Will to Truth*. London: Tavistoc Publications.

— (1980c). 'Power/knowledge'. Gordon, C. (ed.), *Power/Knowledge; Selected Interviews and Other Writings, 1972–1977.* Brighton: Harvester Press.

— (1982). 'The subject and power'. In Dreyfus, H. and Rabinow, P. Brighton (eds), *Michel Foucault: Beyond Structuralism and Hermeneutics.* Harvester Press.

— (1979a). 'Governmentabilty'. *Ideology and Consciousness*, 6, 5–21.

— (1979b). *History of Sexuality,* Vol. 1. NewYork: Patheon Books.

— (1978). 'Politics and the study of discourse'. *Ideology and Consciousness*, 3, 7–26.

— (1977a). *Discipline and Punish: The Birth of the Prison.* New York: Pantheon Books.

— (1977b). 'Nietzsche, genealogy, history'. In Bouchard, D. F. (ed.), *Language, Counter–Meaning, Practice: Selected Essays and Interviews.* Ithaca, NY: Cornell University Press.

— (1973). *The Birth of the Clinic: An Archaeology of Medical Perception.* London: Tavistock.

Frazer, D. and Shields, C. (2010). 'Leaders' roles in disrupting dominant discourses and promoting inclusion'. In Edmunds, A. and Macmillan, R. (eds), *Leadership for Inclusion*, pp. 7–18. Rotterdam: Sense Publishers.

Freire, P. (1970). *Pedagogy of the Oppressed.* New York: Seabury.

Fuchs, D. and Fuchs, L. (1994). 'Inclusive schools movement and the radicalisation of special education reform'. *Exceptional Children,* 60(4), 294–309.

Fulcher, G. (1999). *Disabling Policies?: A Comparative Approach to Education Policy and Disability.* London: The Falmer Press.

Fulcher, G. (1990). 'The politics of integration policy: Its nature and effects'. In Jones N. (ed.), *Review of Special Educational Needs,* Vol. 3. London: Falmer Press.

Furlong, J. (2008). 'Making teaching a 21st century profession: Tony Blair's big prize'. *Oxford Review of Education,* 34(6), 727–39.

Gabel, S. (2002). 'Some conceptual problems with critical pedagogy'. *Curriculum Inquiry*, 32(2), 177–201.

Gale, T. (2001). 'Critical policy sociology: historiography, archaeology and genealogy as methods of policy analysis'. *Journal of Education Policy* 16(5), 379–93.

Gallacher, D. (2001). 'Neutrality as a moral standpoint, conceptual confusion and the full inclusion debate'. *Disability and Society*, 16(5), 637–54.

Gallagher, D. J. (2006). 'If not absolute objectivity, then what? A reply to Kauffman and Sasso'. *Exceptionality*, 14(2), 91–107.

Gardner, H. (1983). *Frames of Mind: The Theory of Multiple Intelligences*. New York: Basic Books.

Gibson, S. and Haynes, J. (2009). 'Introduction'. In Gibson, S. and Haynes, J. (eds), *Perspectives on Participation and Inclusion*. Engaging Education. London: Continuum.

Giddens, A. (1998). *The Third Way: The Renewal of Social Democracy*, pp. 1–18. Cambridge: Polity Press.

— (1986). *The Constitution of Society*. Berkley: University of California Press.

Giroux, H. (2003). 'Public pedagogy and the politics of resistance: Notes on a critical theory of educational struggle'. *Educational Philosophy and Theory*, 35(1), 5–16.

Giroux, H. (1993). 'Rewriting the politics of identity and difference: Critical pedagogy without illusions'. In *Living Dangerously: Multiculturalism and the Politics of Difference*. New York: Peter Lang.

Giroux, H. (1992). *Border Crossings: Cultural Workers and the Politics of Education*. New York: Routlege.

Goodley, D. (2007). 'Towards socially just pedagogies: Deleuzoguattarian critical disability studies'. *International Journal of Inclusive Education*, 11(2), 317–34.

Goodley, D. and Rapley, M. (2002). 'Changing the subject: Postmodernity and people with "Learning Difficulties"'. In Corker, M. and Shakespeare, T. (eds), *Disability/Postmodernity*. London: Continuum.

Grace, G. (1991). 'Welfare labourism versus the New Right: The struggle in New Zealand's education policy'. *International Studies in Sociology of Education*, 1, 25–42.

Graham, L. (2006). 'The politics of ADHD', Paper presented at AARE, November 2006, Adelaide.

— (2005). 'The incidental "Other": A Foucauldian interrogations of educational policy effects'. Proceedings: American Educational Research Association, Montreal.

Graham, L. and Jahnukainen, M. (2011). 'Wherefore art thou, inclusion?: Analyzing the development of inclusive education in New South Wales, Alberta and Finland'. *Journal of Education Policy*, 26(2), 263–88.

Graham, L. and Sweller, N. (2011). 'The Inclusion Lottery: who's in and who's out? Tracking inclusion and exclusion in New South Wales government schools', *International Journal of Inclusive Education*, First published on: 23 February 2011.

Graham, L. J. and Slee, R. (2008a). 'An illusory interiority: Interrogating the discourse/s of inclusion', *Educational Philosophy and Theory*, 40(2), 277–92.

— (2008b) 'Inclusion?' In Gabel, S. L. and Danforth, S. (eds), *Disability and the Politics of Education: An International Reader*, pp. 81–100. New York: Peter Lang.

Green, A. (2002). 'Education, Globalisation and the Role of Comparative Research'. Professorial lecture, Institute of Education, University of London.

Grench, S. (2011) 'Recolonising debates or perpetuated coloniality? Decentring the spaces of disability, development and community in the global South', *International Journal of Inclusive Education*, 15(1), 87–100.

Gutting, G. (1994). 'Foucault and the history of madness'. In Gutting G. (ed.), *The Cambridge Companion to Foucault*. Cambridge: Cambridge University Press.

Halpin, D. and Troyna B. (1995). 'The politics of education policy borrowing'. *Comparative Education*. 31(3), 303–10.

Harwood, V. and Humphry, N. (2008). 'Taking exception: Discourses of exceptionality and the invocation of the "Ideal"'. In Gabel, S. and Danforth, S. (eds), *Disability and the Politics of Education*, pp. 371–384. New York: Peter Lang.

Hindess, B. (1986). 'Actors and social relations'. In Wardell, M. and Stephen, T. (eds), *Sociological Theory in Transition*. Boston: Allen and Umwin.

HMSO (2001). 'Special Educational Needs and Disability Act'. London: HMSO.

Hollenweger, J. (2008). 'Cross–National comparisons of special education classification systems'. In Florian, L. and McLaughlin, M. (eds), *Disability Classification in Education*, pp. 11–30. London: Sage.

Howie, D. (2010). 'A comparative study of the positioning of children with special educational needs in the legislation of Britiain, New Zealand and the Republic of Ireland'. *International Journal of Inclusive Education*, 14(8), 755–76.

Howes, A., Davies, S. M. B. and Fox, S. (2009). *Improving the Context for Inclusion: Personalising Teacher Development Through Collaborative Action Research*. London: Routledge

Howley, M. and Rose, R. (2007). *Special Educational Needs in Inclusive Primary Classrooms*. London; Sage.

Hughes, B. (2005). 'What can a Foucauldian analysis contribute to disability theory?' In Tremain, S. (ed.), *Foucault and the Government of Disability*, pp. 78–92. Michigan, IL: University of Michigan Press.

Humes, W. and Bryce, T. (2003). 'Poststructuralism and policy research in Education'. *Journal of Education Policy*, 18(2), 175–87.

Humphrey, J. (2000). 'Researching disability politics, or some problems with the social model in practice'. *Disability and Society*. 15(1), 63–85.

Janks, H. (1997). 'Critical discourse analysis as a research tool'. *Discourse: Studies in the Cultural Politics of Education*, 18(3), 329–41.

Jordan, A., Lindsay, L. and Stanovich, P. J. (1997). 'Classroom teachers' instructional interactions with students who are exceptional, at risk and typically achieving'. *Remedial and Special Education*, 18, 82–93.

Jordan, R. and Powell, S. (1995). *Understanding and Teaching Children with Autism*. Chichester: Wiley.

Karlsen, G. E. (2000). 'Decentralised centralism: framework for a better understanding of governance in the field of education'. *Journal of Education Policy*, 15(5), 525–38.

Kauffman, J. M. and Hallahan, D. P. (eds). (1995). *The Illusion of Full Inclusion: A Comprehensive Critique of a Current Special Education Bandwagon*. Austin TX: Pro-Ed.

Kauffman, J. M. and Sasso, G. M. (2006). 'Rejoinder: Certainty, doubt, and the reduction of uncertainty'. *Exceptionality*, 14(2), 109–20.

Kendall, G. and Wickham, G. (1999). *Using Foucault's Methods*, London: Sage Piblications.

Kenworthy, J. and Whittaker J. (2000). 'Anything to declare? The struggle for Inclusive Education and Children's Rights'. *Disability and Society*, 15(2), 219–31.

Kirp, D. (1982). 'Professionalization as a policy choice: British special education in comparative perspective'. *World Politics*, 34(2), 137–74.

Kress, G. (1990). 'Critical discourse analysis'. *Annual Review of Applied Linguistics*, 11, 84–99.

Leonardo, Z. (2003). 'Discourse and critique: Outlines of a poststructural theory of ideology'. *Journal of Education Policy,* 18(2), 203–14.

Levin, B. (1998). 'An epidemic of education policy: (What) can we learn from each other?' *Comparative Education,* 34(2), 131–41.

— (1985). 'Equal educational opportunity for children with special needs: The federal role in Australia'. *Law and Contemporary Problems,* 48(2), 213–73.

Liasidou, A. (2011). 'Special education policy making; A discursive analytic approach'. *Educational Policy,* 25(6), 887–907.

— (2009). Critical policy research and special education policymaking: A policy trajectory approach. *Journal for Critical Education Policy Studies,* 7(1), 107–30.

— (2008a). 'Critical discourse analysis and inclusive educational policymaking: The power to exclude'. *Journal of Education Policy,* 13(5), 483–500.

— (2008b). 'Politics of inclusive education policymaking', *International Journal of Inclusive* Education, 12(3), 229–41.

— (2007). 'Inclusive education policies and the feasibility of educational change: The case of Cyprus', *International Studies in Sociology of Education,* 17(4), 329–47.

Liasidou, A. (2009). Critical policy research and special education policymaking: A policy trajectory approach. *Journal for Critical Education Policy Studies,* 7(1), 107–30.

Liasidou, A. and Svensson, C. (2011). 'Theorizing educational change within the context of inclusion'. In Cornwall, J. and Graham-Matheson, L. (eds), *Leading on Inclusion: Dilemmas, Debates and New Perspectives,* London: Routledge.

Lindsay, G. (2003). 'Inclusive education: A critical perspective', *British Journal of Special Education,* 30(1), 3–12.

— (1997). 'Values and Legislation'. In Lindsay, G. and Thopson, D. (eds), *Values into Practice in Special Education.* London: David Fulton.

Lindsay, G. and Thompson, D. (eds) (1997). *Values into Practice in Special Education.* London: David Fulton.

Lingard, B., Knight, J. and Porter, P. (eds) (1993). *Schooling Reform in Hard Times.* London: The Falmer Press.

Lingard, B and Mills, M. (2007). 'Pedagogies making a difference: Issues of social justice and inclusion'. *International Journal of Inclusive Education,* 11(3), 233–44.

Lingard, B. and Rawolle, Sh. and Taylor, S. (2005). 'Globalising policy sociology in education: working with Bourdieu'. *Journal of Education Policy,* 20(6), 759–77.

Lloyd, C. (2008). 'Removing barriers to achievement: A strategy for inclusion or exclusion?' *International Journal of Inclusive Education,* 12(2), 221–36.

Long, M., Wood, C., Littleton, K., Passenger, T. and Sheehy, K. (2011). *The Psychology of Education.* London: Routledge.

Low, C. (1997). 'Is inclusivism possible?' *European Journal of Special Needs Education,* 12(1), 71–9.

Loxley, A. and Thomas, G. (2001). 'Neo–conservatives, neo–liberals, the new left and inclusion: Stirring the pot'. *Cambridge Journal of Education,* 31, 291–301.

Loxley, A. and Thomas, G. (1997). 'From inclusive policy to the exclusive real world: an international review'. *Disability and Society*, 12(2), 273–91.

Luke, A. (2002). 'Beyond science and ideology critique: Developments in critical discourse analysis'. *Annual Review of Applied Linguistics*, 22, 96–110.

— (1996). 'Text and discourse in education. An introduction to critical discourse analysis'. *Review of Research*, 21, 3–47.

Lunt, L. (1998). 'Values of professional groups dealing with children with special educational needs'. In Lindsay, G. and Thompson, D. (eds), *Values into Practice in Special Education*. London: David Fulton.

MacBeath, J., Galton, M., Steward, S., MacBeath, A. and Page, C. (2002). 'The costs of inclusion: NUT report'. University of Cambridge. Available online at http://www.educ.cam.ac.uk/people/staff/galton/Costs_of_Inclusion_Final.pdf.

Macey, D. (1994). *The Lives of Foucault*. New York: Vintage.

MacKay, G. (2002). 'The disappearance of disability? Thoughts on a changing culture'. *British Journal of Special Education*, 29(4), 159–63.

MacLure, M. (1994). 'Language and Discourse: The embrace of uncertainty'. *British Journal of Sociology of Education*, 15 (2), 283–300.

Makkonen, T.(2002). 'Multiple, compound and intersectional discrimination: Bringing the experiences of the most marginalized to the fore', Institute For Human Rights, Åbo Akademi University, April 2002.

Marsh, J. (2003). *Funding Inclusive Education: The Economic Realities*. England: Ashgate Press.

Marshall, C. and Patterson, J. (2002). 'Confounded policies: Implementing site-based management and special education policy reforms'. *Educational Policy*, 16(3), 351–86.

Marshall, J. (1996). *Michel Foucault: Personal Autonomy and Education*. London: Kluwer Academy Public.

— (1990). Foucault and educational research. In Ball, S. (ed.), *Foucault and Education. Disciplines and knowledge*. London: Roultledge.

McDonnell, P. (2003). 'Developments in special education in Ireland: Deep structures and policy making'. *International Journal of Inclusive Education*, 7(3), 259–69.

McGuire, J. M., Scott, S. and Shaw, S. (2006). 'Universal design and its application in educational environments'. *Remedial and Special Education*, 27(3), 166–75.

Mackenzie, S. (2007). 'A review of recent developments in the role of the SENCo in the UK'. *British Journal of Special Education*, 34(4), 212–18.

McLaren, P. (1998). *Life in Schools: An Introduction to Critical Pedagogy in the Foundation of Education* (3rd edn). New York: Longman.

McLaughlin, M. (2009). *What Every Principal Needs to Know About Special Education*. California: Corwin Press.

McWhorter, L. (2005). 'Foreword'. In Tremain, S. (ed.), *Foucault and the Government of Disability*. Michigan, IL: The University of Michigan Press.

Mehan, H. (1984). 'Institutional decision making'. In Rogoff, L. (ed.), *Everyday Cognition: Its Development in Social Contexts*. Massachusette: Harvard University Press.

Mesibov, G. and Howley, M. (2003). *Accessing the Curriculum for Pupils with Autistic Spectrum Disorders: Using the TEACCH Programme to Help Inclusion*. London: Dave Fulton Publishers.

Miles, M. (2007). 'International strategies for disability-related work in developing countries: Historical, modern and critical reflections'. Available online at http:// www.independentliving.org/docs7/miles200701.html (Accessed 21st July 2011).

Mills, C. W. (1961). *The Sociological Imagination*. New York: Grove Press.

Mills, S. (1997). *Discourse*. London: Routledge.

Mitchell, D. (2008). *What Really Works in Special and Inclusive Education. Using Evidence-Based Teaching Strategies*. London: Routledge.

Mittler, P. (2000). *Working Towards Inclusive Education: Social Contexts*. London: David Fulton.

— (1999). 'Equal opporunities for whom?' *British Journal of Special Education*, 26(1), 3–7.

Morris, J. (1996). *Encounters with Strangers: Feminism and Disability*. London: The Women's Press.

— (1991). *Pride Against Prejudice: Transforming Attitudes to Disability*. London: The Women's Press.

Morton, M. and Gibson, P. (2003). 'The rhetoric and practice for partnership: Experiences in the context of disability'. Paper presented at Connecting Policy Research and Practice: The social policy Research and evaluation Conference, Ministry of Social Development, Wellinghton Convention Centre, 29–30, April 2003.

Neave, G. (1977). *Equality, Ideology and Educational Policy: An Essay in the History of Ideas*. Amsterdam: Foundation Europèene de la Culture.

Nguyen, P. M., Elliott, J. G., Terlouw, C. and Pilot, A. (2009). 'Neocolonialism in education: Cooperative learning in an Asian context'. *Comparative Education*, 45(1), 109–30.

Norwich, B. (2010). 'A Response to special educational needs: A new look'. In Terzi, L. (ed.), *Special Educational Needs: A New Look*, pp. 47–111. London: Continuum.

— (2009). 'Dilemmas of difference and the identification of special educational needs/disability: International perspectives'. *British Educational Research Journal*, 35(3), 447–67.

— (2008a). *Dilemmas of Difference, Inclusion, and Disability*. London: Routledge.

— (2008b) 'Perspectives and purposes of disability classification systems: Implications for teachers and curriculum and pedagogy'. In Florian, L. and McLaughlin, M. (eds), *Disability Classification in Education*, pp. 131–149. UK: Sage.

— (2002). 'Education, inclusion and individual differences: Recognizing and resolving dilemmas'. *British Educational Research Journal*, 50(40), 482–502.

— (2000). 'Inclusion in education. from concepts, values and critique to practice'. In Daniels, H. (ed.), *Special Education Re-Formed. Beyond Rhetoric?*, pp. 5–30. London: Falmer Press.

— (1996). 'Special needs education or education for all: connective specialization and ideological impurity'. *British Journal of Special Education*, 23(3), 100–4.

Norwich, B. and Lewis, A. (2007). 'How specialized is teaching children with disabilities and difficulties?' *Journal of Curriculum Studies*, 39(2), 127–50.

— (2001). 'Mapping a pedagogy for special educational needs'. *British Educational Research Journal*, 27(3), 314–29.

Ochs, K. and Phllips, D. (2004). 'Educational policy-borrowing: Historical perspectives'. In Phillips, D. and Ochs, K. (eds), *Educational Policy-Borrowing: Historical Perspectives*. UK: Symposium books.

OFSTED (2005). 'Managing Challenging Behaviour'. London: HMI.

Oliver, M. (1999). 'Capitalism, disability and ideology: A materialist critique of the normalization principle'. First published in Flynn, Robert, J. and Lemay, Raymond, A. *A Quarter-Century of Normalization and Social Role Valorization: Evolution and Impact*. Available online at: http://www.independentliving.org/docs3/oliver99.pdf.

— (1996a). *Understanding Disability: From Theory to Practice*. Hampshire: Palgrave.

— (1996b). 'Defining impairment and disability: Issues at stake'. In Barnes, C. and Mercer, G. (eds), *Exploring the Divide: Illness and Disability*. Leeds, UK: The Disability Press.

— (1990). *The Politics of Disablement*. London: Macmillan.

— (1988). 'The social and political context of educational policy: The case of special needs'. In Barton, L (ed.), *The Politics of Special Needs*. London: Falmer Press.

Oliver, M. and Barnes, C. (1998). *Disabled People and Social Policy: From Exclusion to Inclusion*. Harlow: Addison Wesley Longman.

Olssen, M. (2003). 'Structuralism, poststructuralism, neo-liberalism: Assessing Foucault's legacy'. *Journal of Education Policy*, 18(2), 189–202.

Olssen, M., Godd, J. and O'Neill, M. (2004). *Education Policy: Globalisation, Citizenship and Democracy*. London:Sage.

Office of Public Sector Information (OPSI) (2009). Education (Special Educational Needs Co-ordinators) (England) (Amendment) Regulations 2009. London: OPSI.

Ozga, J. (2000). *Policy Research in Educational Settings: Contested Terrain*. Milton Keynes: Open University Press.

Ozga, J. (1990). 'Policy research and policy theory: A comment on Fitz and Halpin'. *Journal of Education Policy*, 5(4), 359–62.

Ozga, J. (1987). 'Studying education policy trough the lives of the policymakers: An attempt to close the macro-micro gap'. In Walker, S. and Barton, L. (eds), *Changing Policies, Changing Teachers*, pp. 138–50. Great Britain: Open University Press.

Parrish, T. (2000). 'Restructuring special education funding in New York, *Economics of Education Review*, 19, 431–45.

Pather, S. (2007). 'Demystifying inclusion: Implications for more sustainable inclusive practice'. *International Journal of Inclusive Education*, 11(5&6), 627–43.

Pearson, S. (2010). 'The role of special educational needs co-ordinators (SENCOs): "To be or not to be"'. *The Psychology of Education Review*, 34(2), 30–8.

Peter, C. (ed.) (1998). *Managing Inclusive Education: From Policy to Experience*. UK: PCP.

Peters, M. and Humes, W. (2003). 'Editorial: The reception of poststructuralism in educational research and policy'. *Journal of Education Policy*, 18(2), 109–13.

Peters, M. (1999). 'Postmodernism and structuralism: Affinities and theoretical innovations'. *Sociological Research Outline*, 4(3). Available online at http://www.socresonline.org.uk/4/3/peters.html.

Phtiaka, H. (2006). 'From separation to integration: Parental assessment of state intervention', *International Studies in Sociology of Education*, 16(3), 175–89.

Phuong-Mai N., Elliott, J. T., Terlouw, C. and Pilot, A. (2009). 'Neo-colonialism in education: Cooperative learning in an Asian context'. *Comparative Education*, 45(1), 109–30.

Pihlaja, P. (2007). 'Behave yourself! Examining meanings assigned to children with socio-emotional difficulties'. *Disability and Society*, 23(1), 5–15.

Pollard, A. (2008). *Reflective Teaching*. London: Continuum.

Popkewitz, T. and Brennan, M. (1998). 'Restructuring of social and political theory in education: Foucault and the social epistemology of school practices'. In Popkewitz, T. and Brennan, M. (eds), *Foucault's Challenge: Discourse, Knowledge and Power in Education*. New York: Teachers College Press.

Purvis, T. and Hunt, A. (1993). 'Discourse, ideology, discourse, ideology, discourse, ideology . . .' In *Discourse*, 44(3), 473–99.

Quicke, J. (1988). 'The 'New Right' and education', *British Journal of Educational Studies*, 36(1), 5–20.

Ranson, S. (1995). 'Theorizing education policy'. *Journal of Education Policy*, 10(4), 427–48.

Rayner, S. (2009). 'Educational diversity and learning leadership: A proposition, some principles and a model of inclusive leadership'. *Educational Review*, 61(4), 433–77.

Riddell. S., Adler, M., Mordaunt and Farmakopoulou, N. (2000). 'Special educational needs and competing policy frameworks in England and Scotland'. *Journal Education Policy*, 15(6), 621–35.

Rieser, R. (2000). 'Disability discrimination: The final frontier'. In Cole, M. (ed.), *Education, Equality and Human Rights: Issues of Gender, Race, Sexuality, Disability and Social Class*, pp. 118–140. London: Routledge/Falmer.

Rioux, M. (2002). 'Disability, citizenship and rights in a changing world'. In Barnes, C., Oliver, M., Barton, L. (eds), *Disability Studies Today*. Great Britain: Polity.

Rizvi, F. and Lingard. (1996). 'Disability, education and the discourses of justice'. In, Christensen, C. and Rizvi, F. (eds), *Disability and the Dilemmas of Education and Justice*. Great Britain: St. Edmundsbury Press Ltd.

Rix, J., Hall, K., Nind, M., Sheehy, K. and Wearmouth (2009). 'What pedagogical approaches can effectively include children with special educational needs in mainstream classrooms?: A systematic literature review'. *Support for Learning*, 24(2), 86–94.

Roaf, C. and Bines, H. (1989). 'Needs, rights and opportunities in special education'. In Roaf, C. and Bines, H. (eds), *Needs, Rights and Opportunities*. Great Britain: The Falmer Press.

Rose, D. H. (2001). 'Universal design for learning: Deriving guiding principles from networks that learn'. *Journal of Special Education Technology*, 16(1), 66–70.

Rose, D. H. and Meyer, A. (2002). *Teaching Every Student in the Digital Age: Universal Design for Learning*. Alexandria, VA: Association for Supervision and Curriculum Development.

— (2000b). 'Universal design for learning: Associate editor column'. *Journal of Special Education Technology*, 15(1), 67–70.

Ross, J. A. and Berger, M. (2009). 'Equity and leadership: research-based strategies for school leaders'. *School Leadership & Management*, 29(5), 463–76.

Roulstone, A. and Prideaux, S. (2008). 'More policies, greater inclusion?: Exploring the contradictions of New Labour inclusive education policy'. *International Studies in Sociology of Education*, 18(1), 15–29.

Rubinstein, P. (1986). 'The concept of structure in sociology'. In Wardell, S. and Turner, B. (eds), *Social Theory in Transition*. London: Allen and Unwin.

Runswick-Cole, K. (2007). '"The Tribunal was the most stressful thing: More stressful than my son's diagnosis or behaviour": The experiences of families who go to the Special Educational Needs and Disability Tribunal (SENDisT)'. *Disability and Society*, 22(3), 315–28.

Runswick-Cole, K. A. and Hodge, N. (2009). 'Needs or rights? A challenge to the discourse of special education'. *British Journal of Special Education*, 36(4), 198–203.

Rustemier, S. (2002). *Social and Educational Justice: The Human Rights Framework for Inclusion*. Bristol: CSIE.

Rothstein, L. and Jonson, S. (2010). *Special Education Law*. London: Sage.

Sailor, W. and Paul, J. L. (2004). 'Framing positive behavior support in the ongoing discourse concerning the politics of knowledge'. *Journal of Positive Behavior Interventions*, 6(1), 37–49.

Sasso, G. M. (2001). 'The retreat from inquiry and knowledge in special education'. *The Journal of Special Education*, 34(4), 178–93.

Scales, P., Pickering, J., Senior, L., Headely, K., Garner, P. and Boulton, H. (2011). *Continuing Professional Development in the Lifelong Learning Sector*, Maidenhead: McGraw Hill.

Scott, J. (1990). *A Matter of Record: Documentary Sources in Social Research*. Cambridge: Polity.

Scully, L. S. (2002). 'A postmodern disorder: Moral encounters with molecular models of disability'. In Corker, M. and Shakespeare, T. (eds), *Disability/Postmodernity*, pp. 48–61. London: Continuum.

Senior, J and Whybra, J. (2005). *Enrichment Activities for Gifted and Talented Children*. London: Optimus Education.

Shakespeare, T. (1997). 'Cultural representation of disabled people: Dustbins or disavowal?' In Barton, L. and Oliver, M. (eds), *Disability Studies: Past, Present and Future*, pp. 217–233. Leeds: Disability Press.

Shakespeare T. (2006) *Disability Rights and Wrongs*. Oxford: Routledge.

Shakespeare, T. and Watson, N. (2001). 'The social model of disability: An outdated ideology?' In Barnartt, S. N. and Altman, B. M. (eds), *Research in Social Science and Disability, Volume 2, Exploring Theories and Expanding Methodologies*, pp. 9–28. UK: Emerald.

Shapiro, H. (1980). 'Society, ideology and the reform of special education: A study in the limits of educational change'. In *Educational Theory*, 30(3), 211–23.

Shapiro, S. (1989). 'New directions for the sociology of education: Reconstructing the public discourse in education. *Education and Society*, 7(2), 21–37.

Sindelar, P., Shearer, D., Yendol-Hoppey, D. and Liebert, T. (2006). 'The sustainability of inclusive school reform'. *Exceptional Children*, 72(3), 317–31.

Singal, N. and Miles, S. (2009). 'The Education for All and inclusive education debate: Conflict, contradiction or opportunity'. *International Journal of Inclusive Education*, 14 (1), 1–15.

Skrtic, T. (ed.) (1995). *Disability and Democracy. Reconstructing (Special) Education for Postmodernity*. New York: Teachers College, Columbia University.

Skrtic, T. (1991). *Behind Special Education: A Critical Analysis of Professional Culture and School Organization*. USA: Love Publishing Company.

Skrtic, T. M. and Sailor, W. (1996). 'School-linked services integration: Crisis and opportunity in the transition to postmodern society'. *Remedial and Special Education*, 17, 271–83.

Slee, R. (2011). *The Irregular School: Exclusion, Schooling and Inclusive Education*. London: Routledge.

— (2007). 'It's a fit–up! Inclusive education, higher education, policy and the discordant voice'. In Barton, L. and Armstrong, F. (eds), *Policy, Experience and Change: Cross-Cultural Reflections on Inclusive Education.* Dordrecht, Springer.

— (2006). 'Limits to and possibilities for educational reform', *International Journal of Inclusive Education,* 10(2–3), 109–19.

— (2003). 'Teacher education, government and inclusive schooling: The politics of the Faustian Waltz'. In Alln, J. (ed.), *Inclusion, Participation and Democracy: What is the Purpose?* London: Kluwer Academin Publishers.

— (2001a). 'Driven to the margins: Disabled students, inclusive schooling and the politics of possibility'. *Cambridge Journal of Education,* 31(3), 385–97.

— (2001b). 'Social justice and the changing directions in educational research: The case of inclusive education'. *International Journal of Inclusive Education,* 5(2/3), 167–77.

— (2001c). 'Inclusion in Practice: Does practice make perfect?' *Educational Review,* 53(2), 113–23.

— (1998a). 'The politics of theorizing special education'. In Clark, C., Dyson, A., and Millward, A. (eds), *Theorizing Special Education,* pp. 126–136. London: Routledge.

— (1998b). 'Inclusive education? This must signify "New Times" in educational research'. In *British Journal of Educational Studies,* 46(4), 440–54.

— (1997). 'Imported or important theory? Sociological interrogations of disablement and special education'. *British Journal of Sociology of Education,* 18(3), 407–17.

— (1996a). 'Clauses of conditionality: The "reasonable" accommodation of language'. In Barton, L. (ed.), *Disability and Society: Emerging Issues and Insights.* Essex: Longman.

— (1996b). 'Inclusive schooling in Australia? Not yet!' *Cambridge Journal of Education,* 26(1), 19–30.

— (1993). 'The politics of integration – new sites for old practices? *Disability, Handicap and Society,* 8(4), 351–61.

Slee, R. and Allan, J.(2001). 'Excluding the Included: A reconsideration of inclusive education'. *International Studies in Sociology of Education,* 11(2), 173–91.

Slee, R. and Cook, S. (1999). 'The cultural politics of disability, education and the law'. *Discourse,* 20(2), 267–77.

Slee, R. and Weiner, G. (2001). 'Educational reform as a challenge to research genres: Reconsidering school effectiveness research and inclusive schooling'. *School Effectiveness and School Improvement.* 12(9), 83–98.

Sleeter, C. (2008). 'Equity, democracy and neo-liberal assaults on teacher education'. *Teaching and Teacher Education.* 24(8), 1947–57.

Smart, B. (1990). 'Modernity, postmodernity and the present'. In Turner B. (ed.), *Theories of Modernity and Postmodernity,* pp. 14–30. London: Sage.

Squibb, P. (1984). 'A theoretical structuralist approach to special education'. In Barton, L. and Tomlinson, S. (eds), *Special Education Policy, Practices and Social Interests.* London: Croom Helm.

Stainback, S. and Stainback, W. (1998). 'Curriculum in inclusive classrooms: The background'. In Stainback, S. and Stainback, W. (eds), *Inclusion: A Guide for Educators.* Baltimore: Brookes.

Starkey, H. (1991). *The Challenge of Human Rights in Education.* London: Cassel.

Stenson, K. and Watt, P. (1999). 'Governmentality and the 'death of the social': A discourse analysis of local government texts in South-east England'. *Urban Studies,* 36(1), 189–201.

Sullivan, M. (2005). 'Subjected bodies: Paraplegia, rehabitation and the politics of movement'. In Tremain, S. (ed.), *Foucault and the Government of Disability,* pp. 27–44. Michigan, IL: University of Michigan Press.

Sweeting, A. (2001). 'Doing comparative historical education research: Problems and issues from and about Hong Kong'. In K. Watson (ed.) *Doing Comparative Education Research.* United Kingdom: Symposium Books.

Symeonidou. S. (2009). 'Trapped in our past: The price we have to pay for our cultural disability inheritance', *International Journal of Inclusive Education,* 13(6), 565–79.

Szwed, C. (2007). 'Reconsidering the role of the primary special educational needs co-ordinator: Policy, practice and future priorities'. *British Journal of Special Education,* 34(2), 96–104.

Taylor, S. (2004). 'Researching educational policy and change in "new times": Using critical discourse analysis'. *Journal of Educational Policy,* 19(4), 433–51.

— (1997). 'Critical policy analysis: Exploring contexts, texts and consequences'. *Discourse: Studies in the Cultural Politics of Education,* 18(1), 23–35.

TDA - Training and Development Agency for Schools (2007). 'Professional standards for teachers'. London: TDA publications.

Terzi, L. (2010). *Justice and Equality in Education. A Capability Perspective on Disability and Special Educational Needs.* London: Continuum.

Thomas, C. (2004). 'How is disability understood?' *Disability and Society,* 19(6), 569–83.

— (2001). 'Feminism and disability: The theoretical and political significance of the person and the experiential'. In L. Barton (ed.), *Disability, Politics and the Struggle for Change.* London: David Fulton Publishers.

— (1999). *Female Forms.* Buckingham: Open University Press.

— (1997). 'Inclusive schools for an inclusive society'. *British Journal of Special Education,* 24(3), 103–7.

Thomas, G. and Glenny, G. (2002). 'Thinking about inclusion. Whose reason? What evidence'? *International Journal of Inclusive Education,* 6(4), 345–69.

Thomas, G. and Loxley, A. (2001). *Deconstructing Special Education and Constructing Inclusion.* Buckingham: Open University Press.

Thomas, S. (2003). '"The trouble with our schools": A media construction of public discourse on Queensland schools'. *Discourse: Studies in the Cultural Politics of Education,* 24(1), 19–33.

Thomazet, S. (2009). 'From integration to inclusive education: Does changing the terms improve practice?' *International Journal of Inclusive Education,* 13(6), 553–63.

Thompson, D. (1998). 'Value and judgement of school managers'. In Lindsay, G. and Thompson, D. (eds), (1997), *Values into Practice in Special Education.* London: David Fulton.

Thompson, J. B. (1984). *Studies in the Theory of Ideology.* Cambridge: Polity Press.

Thompson, K. (2003). 'Forms of resistance: Foucault on tactical reversal and self-formation'.*Continental Philosophy Review,* 36, 113–18.

Thousand, J., Nevin, A., McNeil, M. and Liston, A. (2006). 'Differentiating instruction in inclusive classrooms: Myth or reality?' Paper Presented at TED/TAM, San Diego, November 2006.

Tomlinson, S. (1982). *A Sociology of Special Education*. London: Routledge and Kegan Paul.

Tomlinson, S. (1985). 'A sociology of special education'. In Thomas, G. and Vaughan, M. (eds) (2004), *Inclusive Education. Readings and Reflections*. London: Open University Press.

Turnbull, H. R. (2009). 'Today's policy contexts from special education and students with specific learning disabilities'. *Learning Disability Quarterly*, 32, 3–9.

Turner, B. (1990). 'Periodization and politics in the postmodern'. In Turner B. (ed.), *Theories of Modernity and Postmodernity*. London: Sage.

Tyler, D. (1997). 'At risk of maladjustment: The problem of child mental health'. In Petersen and Bunton, R. (eds), *Foucault: Health and Medicine*. London: Routledge.

UNESCO (2009). *Inclusive Education*. UNESCO: Paris Available at www.unesco.org/en/inclusive–education/

— (2006). *Plan of Action. World Programme for Human Rights Education*.UNESCO: Paris. Available at www.ohchr.org/Documents/Publications/PActionEducationar.pdf.

— (1994) 'The Salamanca statement and framework for action on special needs education'. World Conference on Special Needs Education, Access and Quality. Available at www.unesco.org/education/educpro/sne/salamanc/index.htm

UN-United Nations (2008). *Convention on the Rights of Persons with Disabilities*. New York: United Nations.

'Union of the Physically Impaired Against Segregation. (1975). 'Fundamental principles of disability'. Leeds University. Available online at: http://www.leeds.ac.uk/disabilitystudies/archiveuk/UPIAS/fundamental%20principles.pdf.

Van Dijk, T. (2001). 'Principles of critical discourse analysis'. In Wetherell, M., Taylor, S. and Yates, S. (eds) *Discourse theory and practice*, 300–18. London: Sage.

Vaughan, M. (2004). '*Inclusive Education: Readings and Reflections*'. London: Open University Press.

Vaughn, S. and Schumm, J. S. (1995). 'Responsible inclusion for students with learning disabilities'. *Journal of Learning Disabilities*, 28(5), 264–70.

Vlachou, A. (2004). 'Education and inclusive policymaking: Implications for research and practice'. *International Journal of Inclusive Education,* 8(1), 3–21.

— (1997). '*Struggles for Inclusive Education*'. Buckingham: Open University Press.

Vongalis-Macrow, A. (2005). 'Displaced agency: Teachers in globalised education systems. Redesigning pedagogy: Research, policy, practice', May 30–June 1, 2005, National Institute of Education, Nanyang Technological University.

Ware, L. (2002). 'A moral conversation on disability: Risking the personal in educational settings'. *Hypatia*, 17(3), 143–72.

— (ed.) (2004). '*Ideology and the Politics of (In) Exclusion*'. New York: Peter Lang.

Warnock, M. (2010). 'Special educational needs: A new look'. In Terzi, L. (ed.), *Special Educational Needs: A New Look*, pp. 32–43. London: Continuum.

—. (2005). '*Special Educational Needs: A New Look*'. London: Philosophy of Education Society of Great Britain Publications, IMPACT SERIES No. 11.

Warnock Committee (1978). 'Special Educational Needs: The Warnock Report'. London: DES.

Watson, K. (2001). 'Introduction: Rethinking the role of comparative education'. In K. Watson (ed.), *Doing Comparative Education Research*, pp. 9–18. Oxford: Symposium.

Watt, J. (1994). *Ideology, Objectivity, and Education*. New York and London: Teachers College, Columbia University.

Weber, Max (1952). *The Protestant Ethic and the Spirit of Capitalism*. New York: Scribner.

Weber, M. (1968). *Economy and Society: An Outline of In-terpretive Sociology*. Three volumes. New York: Bedminster.

Wedell, K. (2008). 'Confusion about inclusion: patching up or system change?' *British Journal of Special Education*, 35(3), 127–35.

— (2005). 'Dilemmas in the quest for inclusion'. *British Journal of Special Education*, 32(1), 3–11.

Welch, A. (1998). 'The cult of efficiency in education: Comparative reflections on the reality and the rhetoric'. *Comparative Education*, 34(2), 157–75.

Westwood, P. (2001). '"Differentiation" as a strategy for inclusive classroom practice: Some difficulties identified'. *Australian Journal of Learning Disabilities*, 6(1), 5–11.

Westwood, P., and Arnold, W. (2004). 'Meeting individual needs with young learners'. *ELT Journal*, 58(4), 375–78.

Whitty, G. (2002). *Making Sense of Education Policy*. Great Britain: Paul Chapman Publishing.

Whitty, G., Power, S., and Halpin, D. (1998). *Devolution and Choice in Education: The School, the State and the Market*. Buckingham: Open University Press.

Wilson, J. (2000). 'Learning difficulties, disability and special needs: Some problems of partisan conceptualisation'. *Disability and Society*, 15(5), 817–24.

Wing, L. (1996). *The Autistic Spectrum*. London: Constable.

Youdell, D. (2006). 'Diversity, inequality, and a poststructural politics for education'. *Discourse*, 27(1), 33–42.

Young, I. M. (1990). *Justice and the Politics of Difference*. Princeton, NG: Princeton University Press.

Young, K. and Mintz, E. (2008). 'A comparison: Difference, dependency and stigmatization in special education and disability studies'. In Gabel, S. and Danforth, S. (eds), *Disability and the Politics of Education*, pp. 499–511. New York: Peter Lang.

Zizek, S. (1994). 'Introduction: The spectre of ideology'. In Zizek, S. (ed.), *Mapping Ideology*. New York: Verso.

Index